Dear God

Published and distributed by Merack Publishing
Jackson, USA
www.merackpublishing.com

Byrd, Melodie
Dear God, It's Me... Again: My Life with My Mother Through Prayers

ISBN
Paperback 978-1-964421-19-3
eBook 978-1-964421-20-9

Dear God

IT'S ME... AGAIN

My Life with My Mother
Through Prayers

Melodie Byrd

I dedicate this book to God.

Also to my sister Miriam, my brother Scott,

my husband Alan, and my daughter Natalie and her family.

Contents

The Early Years

Innocent lives sent out into the world,
Soaking up stimuli, emotions, and words.
Of course we are influenced by those we are near,
But God helps us process whatever we hear.

The miracle of life is our greatest gift,
But those around us can tear down or lift,
Thank You for angels sent from above,
To show us Your protection and everlasting love.

Angels are grandparents, neighbors and friends,
Teachers and churches who gratefully step in.
Wanting to help us nurture and defend,
Yet all that really matters is God's love to the end.

Dear God, it's Me....Again,

Today I was born. It was quite the ordeal. I had known from conception that I was not alone. You created me with an identical twin. We had been getting to know each other for the last eight months. My sister was welcomed to the world first. She was born at 8:02 a.m. One set of nurses whisked her away to get cleaned up and into an oxygen tent. She was blue. Meanwhile, the doctor was working to get me turned around so I too could be born. I was finally born at 8:22a.m. I came out black. I too was whisked off to an oxygen tent. I know it was very difficult on my mom. She does not do well with anything that is out of her control or is painful. It's a good thing she had taken the anesthetic. That's the way they did it back then, for most women.

Mother decided not to bottle feed us since there were two of us. We were sent to the Neonatal Intensive Care Unit (NICU), where they could monitor our breathing and vitals. The nurses said my sister could go home after a week, but I would have to stay a week or two longer until my lungs were working stronger. My grandparents all were coming later today to meet us. There was quite a commotion in the nursery, as identical twins are somewhat of a phenomenon. The nurses were all looking at us and making sure we were all right. We were about 4 weeks premature, and

Each of us weighed a little over 5 lbs. I guess we really did look alike so they put different colors on our wristbands so as not to get us mixed up. So that's how Miriam and Melodie, my sister and I, entered this world. At least God was showing us that we always had each other no matter what would happen in our lives. Each new birth has so much promise as well as uncertainty. You made it clear, God, that You would also be there every step of our journey.

Dear God, it's Me....Again,

It seems like I have been crying for so long now. My eyes are swollen and I am so hungry. The knot in my stomach keeps growing tighter. I want my mommy and I want my bottle. My sister is in her crib crying too. I guess I woke her up or maybe she's just as hungry as I am. I guess I'll go ahead and do what I usually do when this happens. I get on my hands and knees and rock back and forth. It helps me to feel better. It eases the tightness of the knot in my stomach. Then when I get tired of that, I will try crying again. You would think mother or daddy would hear us by now, especially with both of us awake. My sister sees me rocking, so she does it too. After a long while we have both rocked our cribs across the wooden floor. We are both by the door now and we start crying again. Finally, I hear someone trying to open the door to our nursery. It is daddy! We have moved our cribs so far that we are blocking the door. I hear Daddy calling to me. This only makes me cry harder. He pushes and shoves the door a few times and gets one of the cribs to move. I see his hand coming through the crack. He pushes and shoves my sister's crib back from the door. Now finally we will get a bottle. I start to let down my anxiety. I end up having to wait while he feeds my sister first. Where is Mommy? Why can't she feed me? When I finally get my turn, I suck on that bottle so hard my mouth hurts. That warm sweet milk flows down my throat. My eyes are still swollen and I am confused but at least my tummy has stopped aching. After I finish my bottle, my dad lays me back in the crib, which he has returned to its rightful place in the room. I am pretty sure I can go to sleep now. Thank you God, for finally waking my daddy up. I feel myself relaxing for the first time in a long while. It feels good not to be hungry.

Dear God, it's Me.... Again,

Today was a special day. My brother, Scott, was born. I had been waiting so long for him to join the family. I was three. We waited in the main part of the hospital for what seemed like forever. We knew we had to be very good. Our grandma Shephard was coming from Greenville to help watch over us and help with the baby. There was a little gift shop near the elevators, so we went in there and looked around. There were beautiful flowers, stuffed animals, cards and candy to look over. Waiting this much is very hard on two three year olds. We did our best. Across the lobby was the chapel. The nuns that work at the hospital are always coming in and out after their prayers. I went up to the doors and peeked in. It was so beautiful with candles and stained glass windows. I know you heard me praying for mother and Scott. The nurses would often stop to talk to us and sit with us on the bench. It helped to make the time pass. Every time the elevators dinged, I would look for our dad. I wanted him to catch us being good. I think I fell asleep because my sister,

Miriam, poked me awake as my dad got off the elevator. He looks so sad and burdened. Just about then my grandma showed up. They went to the elevator area to talk. They both had tears in their eyes as they hugged each other. My grandma went up on the elevator to be with my mother. Daddy took us to an ice cream shop to get something to eat. We hadn't had anything to eat since breakfast. We ate and we all had ice cream for dessert. He bought each of us a large stuffed animal and he told us what had happened. My mother had a hard time during childbirth. She was okay but would have to stay in the hospital for a few days. Our brother was born with a double cleft lip and palate. He explained that Scott would also have to stay in the hospital to be monitored. He would also have many surgeries over his lifetime. I feel so sorry for daddy. He has so much to do. He has to watch over us, take care of my mom and now take care of Scott. Please God, give him the strength and courage just like you give to me. I love you God

Dear God, it's Me....Again,

My sister and I are going home from the hospital today. We had our tonsils out because we were always getting strep throats and earaches. We got here the night before the operation. The nurses were amazing. They made both of us feel so special by giving us a lot of attention. We got to share a hospital room so that was great. The nurses were parading us down the hallway, and everyone lavished us with praise. I guess just because we were identical twins. They told us that after the operation, we could eat all the ice cream we wanted. They forgot to mention that, afterwards our throats would be very sore. After the operation, one nurse gave Miriam some ginger ale. We were back in our room by then. She said it hurt all the way down to her tummy! We did get a lot of sherbert after that which went down much better. We both like orange sherbert the best. It was nice and comforting to be in the same room. I wasn't scared at all because we had each other. I vaguely remember my mother visiting. Maybe that was right after our surgery, and we were still groggy. We stayed a second night to make sure we were okay. We were. Today we are going home. It feels like mother doesn't like us getting all the attention at the hospital but, I'm not sure why. We felt very safe and cared for at the hospital. We were only four but both of us remember this vividly. Perhaps it was hard on mother to be at the hospital because she had been through many tragic scenes with Scott and herself. Maybe she didn't like the attention we were getting just for being twins. I may not ever know. Thank You God, for always watching over us no matter what the situation.

Dear God, it's Me....Again,

We had the strangest dream last night. I'm about five. In the dream, we were in the backyard playing with our dolls. We were pretending to be great mothers. I was having my doll talk to her doll. Through my doll, I told Miriam about a dream I had remembered.. We lived on a long street which ended at a very busy intersection. In the dream, I was in our car. I was in the back seat waiting for my parents. The car started to roll down toward Main Street. I was terrified we would be killed! My sister stopped me and said that she had had the same dream! We went over it together and all the details were the same. We both had felt that we had no control in this situation and that you, God, were our only hope. We both woke up before we got to the end of the street. I never want to feel that terror again. When we told our mother about the dream, she said it was stupid. She did think it was a strange coincidence that we dreamed the same dream. Thank You again for stepping in to keep us safe.

Dear God, it's Me.....Again,

Hi God, I was wondering about something that mother had us do. She pinned a note onto my sister's shirt and pinned a check onto my shirt. She asked the nine year old boy, who lived on the other side of the double that we lived in, to walk us across the street to the little Convenience Store. I was so confused. I don't understand why she couldn't just go with us? When we got into the store, we went to the owner and had him get the notes. He read it and told us mother wanted cigarettes. He took the check from me. I didn't even know what a check was. He explained it was a way to pay for things. I felt like we were doing something wrong. We weren't allowed to touch our mother's cigarettes at home. The man rolled his eyes and filled in the check's information. He handed the carton to me. He gave all three of us penny candy. We had to wait a long time to cross back over the street. There were so many fast cars. Finally, we made our way back to our house. I was still so uncomfortable about the whole thing. Should we have been asked to do that?

Why didn't mother just walk over with us? At least we got home safely and gave mother the cigarettes she desperately needed. Again, I am confused, God. I love You.

Dear God, it's Me.... Again,

Thank you for sending me into this world with a constant companion. I know you are always there, but somehow you knew I would need someone with skin on beside me to get me through my life. I can't thank you enough for my twin sister. She came into the world first and has been there for me from the minute I was born. I always have someone to talk to, to cry to, to laugh with and to have fun with. We are a source of strength and love to each other. The connection between our hearts is unbreakable and our love unconditional. I know these gifts are from You. People say we can talk to each other without saying a word. We just kind of know what the other is thinking. I'm sure it was not easy for my parents to raise two babies at the same time. We both had to be fed, our diapers changed, our beds made and our clothes washed. I heard daddy say they had to mark down which of us got fed last, so they wouldn't get mixed up. From those rumblings in my stomach, sometimes, I'm not sure if they kept track very well. I hope we are not too much trouble. It is really fun to go out in the double stroller. People are always stopping to talk to us. My mother likes to dress us in the same clothes. She really seems to love the attention that we bring her. I don't know why people can't tell us apart. I don't think we look that much alike. Being a twin is fun. I always have my best friend with me. Sure we fight sometimes like all sisters do, but we never stay mad at each other. Thank you for blessing me with this wonderful person to share my life with, and with love. I know we can get through anything together as long as You are with us, awesome, God.

Dear God, it's Me....Again,

Today was a great day. Miriam and I spent the night with our neighbors, the Gales. They have four children who love to play games and have fun. They take us in a lot when mother is sick or our brother Scott is having an operation. He was born with a cleft lip and palate. It was not easy for my parents. First to raise two twins that came so unexpectedly. They found out my mother was having two babies only a few weeks before we were born, and then a son three years later that would have up to seven or eight surgeries in his lifetime. Thus, there are neighbors and family that are stepping up to help take care of us. So today we played kick the can, tag and hide and seek. It was so much fun to be around them. My sister and I love this family. Mrs. Gale would wash our hair quite often. I wonder if we had lice? She would make great meals and be so kind to us. Mr Gale was so kind and gentle. I never hear him raising his voice. We just felt safe there. My sister and I often fantasize with each other about being a real part of their family. I guess we really are, for now. Their house was always so bright and cheerful. I remember every room of Gale's house, the table where we played cards and games, the living room where we laughed and roughhoused. The kitchen where we help prepare family meals was so warm. Our house always seems so dark. I can only remember the living room and our bedroom. Thank you for sending us to safe places and putting good families in our lives. That is why it's a good day. Next week we will either be at The Gales or the Jewitts, another neighbor with six children. We might be with our grandparents, Grandpa and Grandma Shepherd who lived in Greenville, Ohio. We may never know.

Dear God, it's Me....Again,

What a day! My sister and I are going to kindergarten now. There are no kindergartens in public schools. School starts in first grade here. I guess it must be like this everywhere. My mom calls a cab to pick us up every day. Our family has only one car and my dad uses it to go to work or to find work. He has a hard time finding work. The cab takes us to a nice lady's house. The cab driver is also very nice. There are about 12 other children there for kindergarten too. We hear stories, we are learning our letters, and sounds. We sing tons of songs! We are learning to get along with others and about manners. Once a week we all get to help make a treat in the kitchen. Today we made chocolate chip cookies. Yum! It is so much fun. I know my mother has a lot on her hands these days. Scott is almost two and has had at least three or four surgeries. I think this kindergarten thing may be to give mother a rest and more time with my brother. I know she has a lot of worry and stress taking care of us. We really do try to be good most of the time. We also suspect that Grandma Foster (mother's mom) might be paying for us to come here since she, too, was a kindergarten teacher. She and grandpa live in Akron so she can't teach us. I know if she lived closer, she probably would teach us herself. I like having this routine of coming every day. We now know what to expect and how to act. We have friends to play with and tasks to do. We are never getting yelled at here. I think we may be smarter than I thought because we know how to answer so many questions. I like hearing about math too. It is so logical to add or take away to get answers that don't change. There's always a pattern. I can't wait to get home and tell my mother all about today. Hopefully she will be in a good mood, if she was able to rest. I know this kindergarten thing is going to work out! Thank You, God, for such a great day!

Dear God, it's Me....Again,

Thank you for being there for me last night. I couldn't imagine not having you to talk to. I was so afraid. My parents are screaming and yelling. I just knew someone was going to be hurt. I could feel the tension start to rise in my neck and stomach. They do this so often that you'd think I would get used to it. It usually starts out about money, because we don't have any. Then it usually escalates into name calling and both of them wishing the other were dead. I hope they don't really mean that. My sister and I are huddled in the closet. We had moved into this drafty old house about six months ago, but the rent was cheap. My dad has lost his job again. They were always fighting more when they were stressed. We liked to be away from them during these times so we wouldn't be in the crossfire. This is why my sister and I had built a small altar. The closet had some room.. There was a cross we had made out of sticks and twine, and a bible from our Grandma Foster. We put a vase of flowers on the small table. This was our altar. We put it close to the closet so it was not seen. Sometimes we hid in there ourselves. It was so comforting to have a place to go when the yelling starts. We know we can always talk to You. I know that we are only five, but I am so glad You have given me a twin sister to help me through these times. I know You and Jesus are always there, but it helps to have a human hand to hold on to. We play in the play for hours at a time during the day. If we are good and play without fighting, no one seems to notice us. It is best if we are not noticed because then we don't become the target of an argument. We like to dress up and play house. When we play house, the dolls are our children and are so sweet. They never make anyone mad. They just play and laugh and have fun. We take our dolls to church at the altar. We learned all about You when our grandmother insisted that Mother and Daddy start taking us to church. We don't get to go very often. When we do go on Sundays, it's when my mother is not sick. My grandma Foster goes to her church in Akron every week but she lives far away. We like going to Sunday school and learning all about You and Jesus. At night we use this altar to feel closer to you. When the silence proves to be real, and the tightness slips from my jawline, we sneak back into our beds. Thank You again, for your help last night.

Dear God, it's Me....Again,

I was especially scared last night, when I heard a commotion in my parent's room. I went in to see my dad wrestling with Mom on the bed. They were both yelling at each other and hands and feet were flying everywhere. I couldn't understand what they were so mad about but I could feel the tension in the air like never before. My instincts told me this was worse than usual. I turned on the light and started to cry. My father screamed at me to turn off the light and go back to bed. He said everything was okay. My mother screamed for me to leave the light on and call the police. I didn't know what to do. My stomach felt queasy and my hands were shaking. How could I please them both? It was too hard to make this kind of a decision at seven years old. I compromised by leaving the light on and going back to bed. I lay there under the covers with the blanket pulled over my head. Nausea was growing in my stomach. I wish I could drown out the noise. What if this time one of them really did kill each other? Would it be my fault? I hadn't really obeyed either one. I must not be a very good daughter. I can't seem to please either one. They finally stopped after what seemed an eternity. I lay there frozen, trying not to move a muscle, just in case someone came to check on me. I must have finally dozed off, for when I awoke it was starting to get light outside. The nausea had passed. Wow, we had made it through another night. I wondered if anyone would say anything this morning. Usually no one mentions the nights. We all act like nothing has happened. Sometimes I even wondered if I had been dreaming, but I still had the tooth marks on my hand where I had been biting to keep my teeth from chattering the night before. Sometimes the fighting would be so loud the neighbors would hear. They would often come over or call the police. At least when that happened, I didn't feel so responsible for keeping them both alive. It is hard to understand how people who are supposed to love each other can get this way. I don't understand why they have to fight so much. Don't they understand how frightened it makes me feel? I'm afraid for them, yet I'm also afraid for myself.

At least if they are fighting with each other, I know I am safe for the moment. Last night the police took my mother to the hospital. Daddy said mother would have to be there for quite a while. He called it a breakdown of some kind. That's the first time I consciously remember trying to make myself numb. There were no feelings I could think of that worked. I was too frightened to feel.

Dear God, it's Me....Again,

My dad says my mom is sick. They came and took her away in an ambulance. The sirens and the police and the paramedics frightened me. What was going to happen to us? No one seemed to even notice us off in the corner. We had learned early to stay out of the way, almost invisible. My sister and I had to go to the neighbor's house. We cannot go to see mother where she is. They won't let children go to the rooms. We went with daddy, but could only sit in that dark waiting room while daddy visited her. He called it a State Hospital, but it didn't resemble any hospital I had seen. The walls were dark. There were lots of people sitting around in wheelchairs drooling and making strange sounds. There were bars on the windows and doors. Everyone talked in hushed tones. I was so scared waiting there. I was coloring in a coloring book trying not to feel anything. Sometimes the nurses would come by and say nice things to us. People always notice us because we were twins, and would be dressed alike and look alike too. Daddy said they wouldn't let us see mother, but he would tell her we said, " hi". He went off down that long hallway. I sat there and clung to my sister's hand. It seemed like it took forever for Daddy to come back. He looked drawn and sad. There was something in his eyes that made me feel pity and anger. Pity that he had to go through this, and anger that he couldn't do more to protect all of us. I don't know how long my mother will have to stay here, but I sure was glad to get out of there and go home. Even when home is scary, at least it's familiar. We only had to go there a few times. Daddy sent us away to stay with our Aunt Betty and Uncle Smokey for a couple of weeks. They were so nice to us. They lived on a farm in Indiana. They had sheep and cows. I always feel so free there. I don't have to worry so much about getting in trouble. We must have acted better there because no one kept yelling at us and telling us how stupid we were. I guess little girls must just behave better on a farm, than in a city. My numbness started to go away. We ended up spending time at the farm almost every summer. My mom wasn't always sick but she often needed a break from us. We put on talent shows with my cousins, played with the cats, and helped feed the animals. It was a place to be ourselves and see how other adults relate to children. You always seem to send people to help us out. For that I will be eternally grateful. One thing I really noticed was that Aunt Betty and Uncle Smokey never seem to fight and they never seem to drink either. Maybe they were just more careful not to do those things in front of us. All I know was it felt like a real home should. We would also go every summer to spend a week with our grandma and grandpa Shepherd in Greenville. This is not the grandma that goes to church every Sunday, but then you know that. This one is the kindest and gentlest person I have ever known. I wish I could live with her all the time. We love going there especially during the week of the county fair. My grandpa grew the best fruits and vegetables in town. He grew tomatoes that were enormous. I will eat them right off the vine like apples. He also had cherry trees and Grandma makes cherry cobbler that is out of this world. Grandpa also raised prize-winning gooseberries. He always entered his vegetable in the competitions at the fair. He would get ribbons and we were so proud of him. These were some of the best times of my life. Unlike at home, I felt like it was okay to be around, to be seen, and to be heard. We would get sent to our other grandma and grandpa in Akron for another week each summer. It wasn't quite as much fun, but grandma always took us swimming. She was very kind too and took us to church. She introduced me to You, God and Jesus. She taught us how to pray. That was, and still is, the best gift I've ever received. I guess mother just couldn't handle us for a whole summer. She was sick a lot. It was okay though, because we would eat well and have fun. Neither of our sets of grandparents drink. I guess that must make a lot of difference.

Dear God, it's Me....Again,

Mother has only been home for a few months. I thought things were going to be better this time. She was really nice to us for a while. We went on picnics as a family and to the park. We played on the swings and went down the slides together. It was really fun. I was just starting to relax and feel like we could be a real family. Then, Here We Go again! There was an especially scary incident this time. It sounded like my mother was really being hurt. Daddy said she had just had too much to drink and didn't know what she was saying. She was crying and cursing and saying she didn't want to live anymore. She was saying awful things about all of us. I guess the neighbors called the police,because they showed up at the door. They talked to Daddy for a long time. I heard him saying something about being out of work and mother not feeling well. I calmed down after that. I finally went to bed but was afraid to go to sleep. It's been a lot of nights laying here trying not to worry and wondering if there is something I can do to make things better. I know You are watching over me, God, but I just can't be too careful. When the yelling stops, I don't know whether to be relieved or more afraid. What if they decide to come after me? I put my thumb in my mouth and clung to my teddy bear. I would try to sleep with one eye open. Thanks for being there, God. You help me finally go to sleep and everything seems to be alright this morning. I don't understand but I'm glad. It seems that if I can make it through until morning no one but my sister and I remember anything that happened the night before. My sister and I, jokingly call it the," peachy keen syndrome ", since everything appears to be Peachy Keen the next day! I have to say this is really confusing,

Dear God, it's Me....Again,

I am so sorry dear God. I know that lying is a sin. I tried to follow your ten commandments. I just feel sick inside. Daddy made me lie to the man at the front door. I had to tell him that no grown-ups were home. He wanted money for something Daddy owed. I was so embarrassed. I feel so ashamed to have lied. Please forgive me. This is not the first time either. When people call on the phone, I have to tell them that Daddy isn't here. I don't know why he can't just talk to them. The one man started yelling at me and telling me that daddy would go to jail if he didn't pay him/. I didn't know what to do. I didn't want Daddy to go to jail. He is the only person who can handle mother when she has too much to drink, except on those nights when daddy drinks too. We were in the grocery store the other day and when we went to check out, the cashier wouldn't take Daddy's check. She said he had had too many bounced checks. I'm not sure what that means but I know we had to leave all the groceries there and go to another store. I guess they didn't know Daddy there, because they let him write a check. We got to keep those groceries. I guess we must have trouble with money. Daddy lost his job again. I heard my mom called the church office to ask for food. A nice lady came and brought us a few bags of groceries. It was great. I get the feeling my parents don't like to ask for help. It is hard to go to sleep at night when your stomach is growling and you are so hungry. We were going to Grandma's every Sunday to have a good dinner. She is so kind-hearted. She sends home things from the garden for us to eat. Thank You for sending such nice people to help us. I promise I will try not to lie anymore

Dear God, it's Me....Again,

Well, daddy moved out of the house this week. My mother has accused him of having an affair with one of the women who helped take care of us. Daddy finally finished his engineering degree by going to night school. I sure don't think he was having an affair. When would he have time? He got a new job at Wright-Patterson Air Force Base in the daytime, he worked a second job at a hardware store, he takes us to the grocery store every week, he tries to keep my mother calm, and he is teaching my sister and I how to cook and do laundry. He went to live next door with a retired professor. I guess he wanted to be close to us kids. He only stayed there for about a month. Mother didn't have anyone to yell at except us kids. so they reconciled and he moved back home. I was so glad! I try to stay out of sight most of the time, around my mother. I never know when she would be really nice or be really mean. This disruption in our household had me on edge 80% of the time. I was pulling out my eyebrows when I felt anxiety. I was rocking myself to sleep at night. It felt like I was always doing something wrong. I threw myself into excelling at school. My teachers' praises were like a calming warm bath. One of my teachers showed me how to breathe deeply to calm down. Thank You, God, for being here for me through all the chaos. I couldn't imagine facing everyday without You. I love You!

Dear God, it's Me....Again,

I am so amazed at how You keep putting caring people in our lives. Mother signed us up for brownies when we were in first grade. Our leader has been an amazing person. Ms Jayne has seven children of her own, so she is so positive and fun to be around. We had amazing opportunities and adventures with our troop. When mother was in her good moods, she would show up at activities and act like Ms Jayne' assistant. Mother would continue to help when she felt good but would not when she was in depression. These two patterns went up and down for years. We went to Girl Scout camp for several years. I think maybe one of our grandparents paid for us. I learned so much about the world by earning badges, doing service projects, and looking at world cultures. We would also spend a lot of time at Ms Jayne's house in the summer. We played outside with her children for hours. Games like Kick the Can, Hide and Seek, Kickball and Dodge ball. We always played at their house while mother was at home with our brother or one of her times in the resting home..

We stayed in the troop through Cadettes, which was through 8th grade. These memories are a highlight of my life. Thank You God, and thank You for sending us Ms Jayne.

Dear God, it's Me....Again,

Here I am asking you for some peace in my life. This last week was a little overwhelming. We moved again to another rental house. We had to pack our things in boxes. Of course we weren't doing it right according to our mother. As usual, everything we did seemed to be wrong. I really hate being yelled at and told I am stupid. I had to say goodbye to my first grade class yesterday. I had just made some friends. We're moving in the middle of the year. My brother had another surgery to complete his palate, and mother had just gotten back from the resting home. She often goes there when she has a breakdown of some kind. Especially after one of Scott's surgeries. I feel like so much is happening all at once, and I have little or no control over any of it. The good news is that this house is so much lighter and brighter than the last one. My room is a lot bigger and is flooded with sun through the front window. There is a rather large alcove in the back of the room near our closet. Miriam and I built a little altar there like we had at the last house.. It is our place to go to be near you. We spend as much time as we can in our room. It's always better to be here, where we feel happy and safe. My brother Scott has a room across the hall. There are lots of holes in one of his walls. Our parents told us that those were bullet holes. What kind of parents say that to 5-year-olds and 8 year olds! I think they were joking, but maybe not. Isn't there enough to be worried about already? We went to our new school and met our teachers. We were in separate classes. I'm a little afraid and timid but I will see how this goes. The school is so much bigger than our old one. The teachers are very nice. This will be a new beginning for both of us. I pray this will be a safe place. Thank You, God.

Dear God, it's Me....Again,

I don't understand what I did wrong this time. My sister and I were taking a bath before getting ready for bed. Daddy had let us buy bath soap in a cylinder that had a roller with which you could draw on your body. It was kind of like putting on deodorant. We had seen it advertised on television . We were laughing and giggling and having a great time. We had rolled our faces,and our arms and legs. Mother came banging into the bathroom telling us to hurry up with our bath. She said we were being way too loud. Then she saw that we had both drawn boobs on our chest. She threw a huge temper tantrum, saying we were nasty little girls! How can you be a nasty girl at seven! She made us wash it off and dry ourselves, while she called for Daddy to bring up the yardstick. We were both crying so much, even though we didn't understand what we had done wrong! We laid on the bed, bare bottoms up to get our wacks. By this time we were having a hard time breathing as we were sobbing so much. I just couldn't understand what had gone wrong? I kept wailing. What did we do? We were seven! It's no wonder I was having so much trouble figuring out what was right or wrong in these situations. Everyone else in our lives always said that we were good and polite. God, thank You for never giving up on me. I love you.

Dear God, it's Me....Again,

I had to wear pants all this week to school. I hate that. I much prefer skirts. I was supposed to do the laundry before I watched any television.. I kept putting it off. I hate going to that basement. It is dark and smells so bad. There are piles of dog feces all over and urine too.. Well my sister and I have to do all the laundry. We are nine now and daddy says we have to take more responsibility. We already do most of the cleaning and the dishes. At least there are two of us. There are piles of clothes down there under the laundry chute. We separate them into darks and lights. We wash them, put them in the dryer, and then fold them into piles for each person. I don't mind doing it except for the smell from all the dog poop. Daddy keeps saying we will go down there together and get it all cleaned up, but that never seems to happen. Mother is here all day. I don't understand why she can't do the laundry or at least let the dogs outside to do their business. I really do not understand why people have to live like this. I hate all the mess. I went to use the flower canister the other day to make gravy and it was so dirty I couldn't even tell from the outside if it was flour or sugar. Anyway, back to why I had to wear pants. Mother came down from her room to get another drink and found me watching television while doing my homework. She was so mad because I'm not supposed to have the television on while I work. Also I had not done the laundry. She flew into a rage, screaming and yelling at me. Usually she shouts that Daddy will beat me when he gets home, but this time she was so irate she grabbed the yardstick and ran after me. I tried to get away but she held my arm. I tried to block the stick from hitting me, but it hurt my hand. When all was said and done I had huge welts all over the backs of my legs. They really stung! I have learned not to cry too much or you just get more, that's with mother. If you don't cry enough with Daddy, then he gives you more. I tell you I am always so confused. I wanted to wear my plum skirt this week. Maybe next week. I did get all the laundry finished after that. I held my nose and tried not to gag. Thanks for letting me vent to You, once again. I couldn't do this without You, God. Schools don't know what is really going on in homes.

Dear God, it's Me....Again,

I am so distressed!. I love her so much. Her name is Missy. She always cheers me up with her loud purring and her loving kisses with that rough tongue. She always lets me cry into her soft fluffy fur when I am sad. I don't know where she has gone. She does go outside sometimes but always shows up for dinner. It has been about a week since I have seen her. My sister and I have been looking everywhere. I am so worried about her. Pets give me such unconditional love. Well, I can get that from You, of course and I do. I can also get that from my sister. Mother doesn't want to get another cat. I wish You would change her mind. I'm rocking and rolling and humming a lot to go to sleep. I always do that when I am anxious and worried. Mother doesn't like that either. I'm trying so hard to forget about Missy. God, maybe I can get another cat someday. I think I'm going to pretend that she is with You, so I won't have to worry so much. It is just one more disappointment in an unstable life. I love You, God. Please watch over her wherever she is.

Dear God, it's Me....Again,

I am so happy to be going to Grandma and Grandpa Shepherd's house. It is Fair week. I think we have come every year since we were five. We get to stay almost two weeks this time. There are so many things to see. We love the animal barns with rabbits, hens, cats, pigs and horses. There are a lot of baby animals too. Some of the 4-H members will let us pet and even hold them. We will also go into the buildings to look at so many kinds of vegetables that were grown by local farmers. Grandpa always gets the price for the biggest and best gooseberries. I'm not sure what they make with gooseberries but he wins every year. We also go through the barn that has quilts and crafts. It is overflowing with beautiful handmade items to look at. There are usually a few carnival rides and games to play in the evening. We will go back to see the show for the night. One night it's horse racing and we watch the horses go around the track pulling buggies. The grandstand gets so loud and exciting. Everyone is cheering for their own team. Another night we will watch the horse riders do dressage with their beautiful horses. That night is much quieter in the stands. I think this year they are also going to host a demolition derby with old cars. They all ride around and crash into other cars. It's really wild! The last car that can still drive is the winner. We love staying with our grandparents, anytime really, but especially during the fair. They are always so nice to us, and we eat really well. We must be better at behaving here also, because no one yells at us and makes us cry. Our brother is not here this week as he is having another surgery on his mouth. I think that is why we are going to stay a little longer this year. A part of me wishes I could live here all the time, but we really need to help out at home. Thank You God, for giving us a great time this year at the fair! I already know we will.

Dear God, it's Me....Again,

Last Night I was awakened at about 2:00 a.m. by the sounds of sirens. There was a huge commotion. The ambulance was there for my mother. The paramedics were putting my mother onto the gurney. She was moaning and I could see some blood. It couldn't have been a fight, because I had heard no yelling and screaming. The three of us children were huddled at the top of the stairs watching what was going on as they took my mother's vitals and assessed her. They took her out to the ambulance. I wasn't sure what was going on. We were so confused. It was right around Christmas time. My dad told us to go back to bed and he called a friend to come to the house so he could go to the hospital to be with my mother. We knew mother was going to have a baby but that was not supposed to happen until after Christmas. The next day my dad came home about lunch time. He was upstairs, when he called all three of us to come to the bathroom. He was sitting naked on the toilet. We were all lined up on the edge of the bathtub. He started to cry as he told us our little brother, Kirk, had passed away. Daddy said Kirk was only alive about 12 hours. There were lots of complications which was why he came so early. He said mother was very tired and upset. She would stay in the hospital a couple more days to help her heal and to grieve. He told us that we all three had to be very good when she came home and not cause her any stress. I feel so sad that we lost him, I genuinely tried to imagine what mother was going through. I'm asking you, God, to help her through this. I will be a great helper when she comes home, because it's almost Christmas time. We're going to get the decorations up and hope it will make her feel better. I cried all afternoon. Poor Kirk. I cried myself to sleep.

Dear God, it's Me....Again,

My grandma, on my mother's side, is coming to visit next weekend. We are all in deep cleaning mode. We usually go up to her house which is in Stow, Ohio, a suburb of Akron. Whenever she does come, mother wants everything to be perfect. We will be working in the kitchen today. It's not a huge kitchen so it shouldn't be too bad, I thought. Well, I started with the aluminum canisters. I could see very little aluminum peeking through. Flour and sugar were caked on the outside of each canister. It took scraping, cleaning with hot water, and lots of rubbing to get them clean and dry. My sister was working on the stove. There was grease and grime and more caked flour on the stove. We learned from our dad how to take the burner covers out and wash them. It took actual scraping to get the burnt debris off. We are both well into the third hour of cleaning. I've moved to the oven which requires spraying all the insides with oven cleaner spray and waiting for it to loosen the baked-on food. Then what seemed like twenty refills of the warm water

Dear God, it's Me...Again

bowl and wet rags to wipe the sides and bottom clean. We took a break and made bologna sandwiches for lunch. The next task will be the sink area and the blue shag carpet that runs through the kitchen area. We did the sink area together and then tackled the floor. I was gagging as I tried to clean the masses of old food and dirt. The water would get so disgusting. I had to take breaks outside in the fresh air. I've always had trouble breathing around too many chemicals. I guess maybe because my lungs were underdeveloped at birth. I really wanted grandma Foster to come. What surprised me was the amount of neglect everywhere in the kitchen. I guess we really didn't see it after being around it so much. Miriam and I were making the meals most of the time now. My dad would cook on the weekend sometimes. My sister and I would cook during the week. We would make grilled cheese and soup, hamburger helper with salad, or fish sticks in the oven. Mother had two famous recipes that she would make if we were having company, her three alarm chili or a pot roast with carrots and potatoes. My dad was the real cook. He had worked in a small restaurant in Illinois that his parents ran during, and after, the Great depression. He could make the best fried chicken with mashed potatoes and gravy. Well, back to the kitchen cleaning. My dad did rent a shampoo washer from the hardware store to go over the shag carpet. It did a pretty good job considering the circumstances. Tomorrow, our room will get cleaned. Grandma always stays in our room when she visits. I hope I get a good night's sleep. You know, I feel a bit of pride at how the kitchen turned out. Not bad for a couple of ten year olds. I hope Grandma will like it. Good night. Dear God.

Dear God, it's Me....Again,

Hi, it's me crying myself to sleep again. Mother made us get our hair all cut off today. My sister and I had hair down to our waist. It was long and thick and wavy. People always complimented us when we were out. It made me feel warm inside even though I was embarrassed to have the attention. She said it was because we wouldn't take care of it but I think she just didn't like to mess with curlers and the tangles. You see every night when I go to sleep, I rock and roll and hum.. I know it sounds kind of weird but it's the only way I can get to sleep. I roll back and forth on the bed and I hum out loud. Sometimes I even get up on all fours and rock back and forth. What's really funny is that my sister does it too. I think I first started it to drown out the sound of my parents fighting, but now it gives me such comfort. I just do it without thinking. I guess I must do it in my sleep too, because when I wake up each morning, I have these large tangled masses in my hair. They are too hard for an eight year old to get them out. Mother has to spray it with a daily detangler and then comb and brush. I know it can be a lot of work. Luckily, my mother doesn't get up every day. On those days, I do my best. I pull it back in a ponytail. I just hate this pixie haircut. It is SO short! Why do we always have to do what is easiest for mother? Well, I guess I will be able to sleep a little longer in the morning. Dear God, do you think if I really try hard to stop rocking back and forth at night and not hum out loud, You could talk mother into letting me grow my hair long again? Well, thanks for listening. I'm really going to work on it. Maybe the short hair will help Mother get up more mornings with us since she won't have to do so much work. This afternoon I overheard my mother talking to a friend. She was telling her that Daddy took my cat to the pound because mother didn't like the fur. Poor Missy. Good night God,. I am so sad tonight.

Dear God, it's Me....Again,

I couldn't wait till bedtime to talk to you, God! Thank You so much for my second grade teacher. She is so kind and gentle. I didn't know that grown ups could be so nice. She listens to me when I have something to say and she makes me feel safe at school. I usually don't say anything in class but this year is different. Her name is Mrs Hess. I am a little upset that my sister is not in my classroom this year. They say it is sometimes good for us to be apart, but I don't like it. I feel lonely enough all the time without having Miriam close by. Maybe this new teacher will help me feel more accepted and less shy. I was riding my bike today at the park next to the Seminary by our house. I saw Mrs. Hess at the door to one of the apartments. Her husband is going to school to be a minister. I waved at her and rode my bike over. She said," hi", and asked how I was doing. She asked me if I wanted to come in for a drink of water. It was a very hot day and I had been riding for hours. I must have looked pretty sweaty and thirsty. I went in and she showed me around the apartment. She showed me some of the paintings she was working on. I couldn't believe it! She was a teacher and an artist! Her place was so neat and tidy. Not at all like our house at home where everything is covered in dust and dog hair. What a wonderful lady. I had never had anyone be so willing to talk to me except my sister. I went home that day feeling so special. When she talks to me she looks at me straight in the eyes. I felt this warm feeling rise through my body. She is really interested in what I have to say. I rode my bike up the street. I felt that feeling again, almost as if I was important. My teacher had taken the time to talk to me and show me where she lives. I knew right then, that I wanted to be a teacher too when I grew up. Please help me to do well in school so I can be just like her. And God, please help her to like me.

Dear God, it's Me....Again,

Mother has a part-time job this summer. Her latest therapist has given her some hours in his office to file papers, answer phones and make calls. She's going to be working about three hours a day, three days a week. This job is at the Theological Seminary fairly close to our house. The three of us children are going with her on those work days. There is a nice playground outside. We are to stay there and play while mother is working. We can only go indoors to use the restroom, get a drink of water, or in case of an emergency. Today is our first day. We like to swing, slide and go on the merry- go- round. There are also a couple of trees to climb. Sounds good. My sister and I are ten, and our brother is seven. Does mother realize how long three hours turned out to be? At least we are outdoors. The weather is good today. I think tomorrow we will bring some books and paper with crayons. Scott is a little bit hard to keep busy. He likes to fill in the time by throwing dirt on us and whining about being hot. I'm not sure what we are supposed to do on rainy days. I guess we will have to work that out. Again it is all about what mother wants. She could have gotten us a babysitter or let us stay home. She does whatever will be the most convenient for her. The good news is that mother never stays at a job for long. She easily gets overwhelmed. I do think she is in a good place and doing something, rather than getting drunk at night and staying in bed all day. That being said, it could be a long hot summer. Please help the rest of the days go fast this summer. I love You, God.

Dear God, it's Me....Again,

School has become a very safe place for me. I feel liked, appreciated, and smart. I am very shy though. I hate being in the spotlight for any reason. I'm starting to feel less scared every day. I can feel a major separation between my life at home and my life at school. I noticed that I'm different at home than I am at school. School has become a place of nurture and growth. There is a consistency at school where actions have consequences and rewards. I feel like the good " me" is at school, and the hidden " me"is at home. Home is so unpredictable! This week we have another babysitter in the house. She is strict and mean. Mother is away again. I walk to and from school every day, and again for lunch. Our school doesn't have a cafeteria. Today when I came home for lunch, I asked for a bologna sandwich. The lady said I could have peanut butter. I shrugged my shoulders. Apparently, that made her mad. She yelled at me and told me I'm ungrateful and naughty. I cried all the way back to school. Is there no one besides teachers and grandparents that are nice?

Where they got this woman, I don't know. She never smiles at us. She's especially mean to my brother. We are afraid for him and ourselves. When mother gets home, I'll bet she won't let her stay. Whoever thought I would prefer mother over this sitter. At least with mother we know what to expect, kind of.

Dear God, it's Me....Again,

I am so scared, God, I don't know what to do. We are on our first family vacation ever. It was supposed to be a lot of fun. We are going to Texas to see some old friends of my mom and dad. We have traveled quite a distance and it hasn't been too bad except for the constant smoking in the front seat. My mom is very nervous and smokes one cigarette after another. Daddy smokes too but not as much. All that smoke goes right into the back seat. My lungs get so full I can hardly breathe. She doesn't like to have her window down because of the wind on her. She keeps it open to crack but it doesn't really help. Anyway, we made it down here to Texas and we were supposed to see the ocean for the first time ever. I was so excited. I finally felt like we were doing something a really normal family would do. When we were about a hundred miles from Galveston, we heard on the radio that there were warnings about a hurricane that might hit land. More people were leaving the city than coming to it. My dad said it would be fine, since those reports were wrong more than they were right. So we kept on driving. It was dark when we got to Galveston and daddy found us a cheap hotel room. He said it was right on the beach but we would have to wait until morning to see the ocean. Us kids were all piled on one bed with Mother and Daddy on the other. I had fallen asleep but was awakened by the howling and screeching of the wind. It was throwing things against our door and rain was coming in through the windows. I started to cry. My sister did too. It was very frightening. I was afraid we would all die. We were only ten and did not understand what was happening. My brother who was seven, seemed to be able to sleep through anything. Mother was telling us to shut up and not be such babies. Daddy was telling us to go back to sleep. He put a Poncho over our bed so we would not get wet. He said everything would be fine in the morning. So I'm lying here trying not to cry and trying to pretend I'm asleep. I am so scared. I have been in so many situations like this where I'm not sure what is happening but this one was not man-made. It doesn't seem to make it any less scary. Please keep us safe tonight, God. If only the wind would stop pounding so loudly. I just wish something could go right for a change. When we woke up the next morning, we were on the other side of the sand wall. The side toward the ocean. We were lucky to be alive. Camilia was a category five hurricane. Thank You, dear God.

Dear God, it's Me....Again,

Here I am again humiliated and frustrated. My sister and I are in third grade this year. Money is tight. There was a church about five houses down from us on our street. Today mother gave us a note to take to the church to see if they could give us some food for the week. As we walked inside, I could feel myself reddening and I could not look the secretary or the minister in the eye. They were very nice and asked us if we had something to carry the food in. We told them we could go get our wagon. We got back with the wagon and they helped us load it up. The minister said to tell our mother he would be coming to call on her in a few days. I didn't know whether to be grateful because we would have food, or melt into the floor, never to be seen again. I'm sure this is connected to last week's grocery shopping episode. We usually go with my dad on Saturdays. Last week we went to pay and it would not accept a check, as the last two had bounced. I was so embarrassed. That was not the first time it had happened. I'm looking forward to going to my

Grandma and Grandpa Shepherd's house on Sunday. She makes the best chicken and noodles. I know we will be full then. She also has snacks for us to take home. You sure put wonderful grandparents in my life. I'm humbled, dear God. I always have thought that You gave us Grandma Foster to teach us about your church, and Grandma Shepherd to show us how to be kind to others and spread Your love. Both grandparents give us unconditional love. Something for which I will always be grateful.

Dear God, it's Me....Again,

I know You saw what happened today. Mother was ranting and raving at us because we were being too loud in the house. We were laughing and giggling while doing our homework. She sent us to our room to wait until daddy came home. That meant that spankings were coming. My Daddy always makes us pull down our pants and lay face down on our beds. I was so terrified because it was almost time for my period to come. What humiliation I felt. I knew You were with me. So thank You for not having my period start. We were told to keep our bedroom doors open at all times, since as far back as I could remember. Also the bathroom door. Miriam and I would just shower after he left for work. He would often walk naked in the house. Today he gave us four wacks with a yardstick. We cried for a long time. I was not crying so much about the pain. It always hurts. My tears were coming from the humiliation, the anger and the circumstances. Crying also helps get out some of my emotions. I just don't know how spanking makes anybody feel better.

Dear God, it's Me....Again,

Oh my gosh! I am gagging so much! I can't get the soap taste out of my mouth. Miriam and I had made cookies for a bake sale for school. We packaged them up in baggies to take to school the next day. We left five cookies out on a plate. There was one for each of us. When it came time for dinner, the cookies were going to be our dessert. We all sat down to dinner and ate our Hamburger Helper that Miriam and I had made with a salad and a can of vegetables. When the plates were cleared, I went out to bring in the cookies. There were only four on the plate. Mother went into one of her rages screaming about who ate the other cookie. She had Daddy line us up in the kitchen and they kept yelling at us. We were all three crying. Each of us said we didn't eat it. So one by one we were taken over to the sink to have our mouths washed out with soap. Daddy put the soap in our mouths and made sure to scrape it over our bottom teeth. The soap was disgusting! They kept saying that since none of us would admit it, we would all get a mouth full of soap because we were lying. We were sent to our bedrooms to think about what we had done. I was miserable. I couldn't stop gagging through my soapy tears. After about a half an hour we were allowed to go into the bathroom and rinse our mouths out. I remember still tasting it the next morning when I was getting ready for school. We never found out who ate the cookie. It could have been my dad or mom but we will never know. Unfortunately this was not the first or last time this would happen.

Dear God, it's Me....Again,

O h please don't make me eat another pancake! This is the third night in a row. I know I should be grateful to have food to eat. You also know how much I hate that feeling of hunger that can grip your body. I've felt that many times before. We will get to go to Grandma's tomorrow and have a good meal after daddy gets off work at the hardware store. He's working there part-time while he looks for a better job. He is an engineer but he never finished College. I don't know why he keeps getting laid off from jobs. Maybe because he takes off so many days after he has too much to drink the night before. He and mother ran off to get married when they were in college. She never finished College either. I'm glad he has some money coming in because he can at least get us some groceries like milk and bread, but I hate the fact that he also can get free yard sticks from the hardware store. That is a favorite thing to hit us with when we've been bad. Mother will chase us around for disturbing her. Screaming and yelling at us because we can't find things to do on our own all day. Summer vacation can be so long. I will be glad when school starts again and

I can be gone all day. Mother gets up at about 11:00 a.m., drinks a pot of coffee, and then sits in her room to write until Daddy comes home. She says she's going to be a great writer someday. She comes down when we have dinner fixed and then the two of them start drinking until bedtime. They call them highballs. What an odd name for a drink. I don't know what she does that is so important that we can never interrupt her. Well, that brings me back to dinner. Pancakes again, with that awful syrup made from brown sugar and water. Maybe I'm a bad child for complaining. At least when Daddy was totally out of work, the church down the street brought us some good food. I love fried spam. I will just try to be grateful and wait until tomorrow. I hope Grandma will make her chicken and noodles! The best part is, at her house, we get to help her in the kitchen and set the table. She talks to us and loves for us to come and visit.

Sorry God, for being so ungrateful for pancakes.

Dear God, it's Me....Again,

I am so totally embarrassed! How can I ever walk down the streets again? We just got back from visiting my grandma in Akron for the weekend. We were unloading the car and I turned to see my dad going to the neighbor's house. He talked to them and then went to the next neighbor. What was he doing? At about the third house the neighbor went inside and came back out with a bottle of booze! Here my mom had sent him to get her some alcohol because we didn't have any and it was a Sunday. They didn't sell alcohol here in our state on Sundays. It's one thing to know in your own home what is going on, but to have all the neighbors know? I went to my room and cried. Why did I have to be in this family? I have to walk to school tomorrow passing all these houses and neighbors, and now they all know. I have spent so much of my life with my head down. I go to school and try not to be noticed. I use so much energy to convince myself and those around me that what I live with is normal. Maybe they won't get it. No, this probably just helps to explain all the times my mom has screamed at different neighbors for petty little things.

When Mother drinks she can be so mean. I guess I was hoping we could contain the madness inside the house. Sometimes we look like such a nice family from the outside, with three children and a dog. Just like Ozzie and Harriet. Who am I kidding? You know the truth, and have all along. Please help me through this latest humiliation. Maybe if I walk with my head down I will never have to look any of these neighbors in the eye. I feel like I've spent half my life with my head down. I'm in high school. I am so conflicted. Half the time I feel like the adult in the family, cooking, cleaning, trying to keep everyone happy. Then I go to school and try not to be noticed. I just want to blend in, be low key. I feel sick inside every time the attention is turned on me. There's enough drama at home. The calm of no chaos is so comforting. You are comforting me also. Another day, another drama.

Dear God, it's Me....Again,

Please dear God, help me to be grateful. Daddy has had a steady job with the government for a while now. We are eating well and mother has not been taken away for quite some time. They decided to buy a camper for us all to go camping in the summer. It was a pop-up camper and it was very nice. Each weekend we go though, has become a disaster. I don't know why I keep expecting anything else. Just because mother is in one of her "involved" phases, doesn't mean we are the Cleavers. Mother does help get things ready, like the food and stuff, but when we get there to set up the camper, she refuses to help. She will start and then wait for Daddy to say one thing wrong. It starts an argument and she will refuse to help from then on. Us kids and Daddy, end up doing all the work of setting up the poles, leveling the camper, setting up the dining fly and making camp. Then she will make up with Daddy and they will pop open the beer and start the drinking. This goes on the entire weekend. I enjoy being away and from home but I hate being out in a semi-public place with them drinking and fighting all the time. People who are campers seem to like to hang out together and share stories and sit around the campfire. It was fun when we were all in a good mood. I just hate always feeling like I'm on pins and needles waiting for one of them to pick a fight or get so drunk that they take it out on us. Or worse yet, unsuspecting fellow campers. My nerves are always on edge. I can feel the hairs on the back of my neck stand up when my mother starts to laugh a little too loud. I know I should be more accepting but I am in high school and even normal parents can be embarrassed to their children at this age. It's just with them, everything is so unpredictable. Take tonight for example, we were camping with this other family and things were going well until mother decided that suddenly us kids were being too noisy. She had had a few drinks and started screaming at us about how annoying we were and how we only ever thought of ourselves. She said for the 100th time in our lives that, " children should be seen and not heard". Now none of this is surprising to me but the embarrassment is what is so overwhelming. I feel like a total idiot. I really wanted to just run away or throw one of the beer cans in her face. Instead I went into the camper and went to bed.

Even though it was only nine pm. I cried myself to sleep, something I do often these days. Please help me to be more tolerant. We have hardly ever gotten to go anywhere away from home and it is great to be outdoors and be able to swim in the lake and eat s'mores around the campfire. I'm asking you again for patience and understanding. I will keep trying to be less annoying to her. Good night God.

Dear God, it's Me....Again,

My Dad is a bully! He doesn't have much control over mother, so he takes his anger out on those around him. Often it was aimed at the three of us, Miriam, Scott, and myself.. He would yell at the manager of the grocery when they wouldn't take a check. That was because so many had already bounced. Our name was on a list at each check out register. On the few occasions we did eat out, he would yell at the waiters or the staff about the order being messed up or the food not being cooked right. Eight times out of ten he would get the meal for free or at least some money off the bill. Always while we were sitting there totally embarrassed. I couldn't look at the waiters or the people sitting around us. I could feel my face growing redder and redder. The tears would spill over from my eyes. I would start pulling out my eyebrow hairs or rocking in my seat to try and calm my anxiety and embarrassment. In our teen years, daddy would make fun of our bodies. He told my sister that she looks slutty for rolling up her skirt at the waist. He told me that no matter how much makeup I had on, I couldn't hide my acne. He made me add material to a bathing suit I had made because my belly button showed. It is the seventies! The thing I hate the most though, is what happened again today. It is why I have brought up all this. He keeps taking only me when he runs errands. Then he starts telling me details of his sex life with mother. I'm only a kid! I don't want to hear all his complaining. He said he just needs someone to talk to. God why does he have to tell me? I listen but I'm so anxious. My knees and my legs are shaking. I just want to go back home. He's done this a few times and I hate it. It feels like he's bullying me into listening to him. Please God, help me find excuses to not be able to go the next time that he asks.

The Teens and Twenties

With teenage years are changes
On the inside and the out,
Wondering where their destiny is
And what the future will be about.

As each of these years pass us,
It changes who we will be.
We try new things, some fail and some win,
God guiding me to be me.

As we find ourselves in adulthood,
Creating our lives anew,
We slowly build a steady life
To reveal our plan to You.

Dear God, it's Me....Again,

Why do I feel so ugly? I know I'm your creation, yet I feel so awful. My skin is all broken out and my teeth are in braces, and I have to wear glasses. I would love to have contacts but we can't afford them. The only reason we have braces is because grandma is helping to pay for them and the orthodontist felt sorry for my parents having to put two kids through braces at the same time. He gave us a price break. Daddy has a job right now. I know it is like that for hundreds of other teenagers, yet I can't help but feel I am the only one who feels so fat and ugly. I hate for people to look at me. I'm so shy and scared all the time. This just doesn't seem fair. School is the only place I ever felt close to normal and now these teenage years have converged on me. It's almost like a conspiracy to see where I can feel worse now, school or home. At least school used to be a safe place and I knew nothing bad was going to happen for at least six hours of the day. Today I felt so bad about myself, I ran into the bathroom at the change of classes. I hid in the stall until right before the bell rang, so I wouldn't have to pass so many people in the hall. I slipped into a seat at the back of the room and hoped no one would notice me. I know being a 14-year-old is no picnic. I just want to look in the mirror and see something close to pretty. I am 5'6" and weigh 125 pounds. I have long dark hair, and hazel eyes. That doesn't sound so bad yet all I can see are my flaws. I see acne on my face, my glasses, my buck teeth with braces, my frizzy wavy hair, my big nose and my small lips! I keep hearing those quotes from home that say I am lazy and good for nothing and that I will never amount to anything. Please dear God, help me to feel better about myself. I'm sure it doesn't help that my sister and I are made fun of at home constantly. The other night, Daddy said to my sister, that her butt was getting so big it looked like she had," secretary "spread." He told me my glasses look like Coke bottles too. He thinks he's trying to be funny but I'm not exactly laughing. I get good grades. I work hard at school and at home. I don't understand why I can't seem to hold my head up and be just who I am. Maybe because I'm not really sure who I am. I wonder if life is this hard for everyone?

Dear God, it's Me....Again,

I am so angry!!. I was at my friend's house last night to spend the night. My sister was with me. p My friend's dad is a minister at our church. He is so kind and gentle. Sometimes I think You bring these special people into my life just so I won't go crazy. He runs our youth group at church. .My sister and I had been there all evening, hanging out with their normal family. The family decided to go out for pizza. That was great with me because we hardly ever got pizza. There were a lot of times we had to eat cereal or whatever we could find for dinner. We went and had a great time period. Their family is so fun to be around because they tell jokes and stories all the time to each other. After we got back to their house and got inside,, there was a knock on the door. It was my dad. He barged in bellowing. "Where have you been?" I told him the family had gone out for pizza. He said, my sister and I were not where we said we would be, so we had to get my things and come home now..He said my mother had sent him over because she had tried to call me and I wasn't there. My friend's dad tried to explain, but my dad said I should have called to tell them where we were going.. It was my fault. Everything is always my fault. I cannot seem to do anything right. He told the minister that I had lied and could not be trusted. I was so humiliated and angry. I was with adults! It's not like I had snuck out of the house..My mom had probably been drinking and wanted to call and tell me how mean my dad was being to her. When I wasn't there, she got mad. She liked to put us girls in the middle. It almost seems like we are supposed to protect her rather than the other way around. Gee, God, life seems so unfair. No wonder I didn't make too many friends. I'm afraid my mom and dad will embarrass me in front of them just like they have tonight. My mother and daddy won't even go to this church with us except on Christmas and Easter.. My sister and I started going this year, because the girl in my home room invited me. If they would come more often, they would know how nice the minister and his daughter are. I am so livid!!!

Dear God, it's Me....Again,

I can't believe it. I am lying here afraid to go to sleep again. I am so sure my mother will try to kill me tonight. I know it was wrong of me to get into a fight with my dad. I am seventeen years old and I should have a right to say who my friends are. I know it is not right to raise your voice to a parent but I was so mad! My dad hit me so hard across the face that his wedding ring came off and flew across the room. I guess I went way too far. The worst part is that he went and told my mother that I slapped the ring off His finger when he was defending himself from me trying to hit him! What a downright lie! It's hard enough to figure out reality around here but to twist the truth so completely around just makes me sick deep inside. Then my mother who had been drinking all evening as usual, came and screamed at me, calling me every name in the book for disrespecting my father and said she wished I was dead. Now here I am laying in my room at 2:00 in the morning, afraid to go to sleep for fear she is going to come in and kill me. I'm so tired of living like this. I know you will protect me but honestly, when she is so far gone, I'm not sure even You could step in. I don't think she could stop herself. I want to leave and just run away. I called and talked to Grandma about leaving the other day but she said to hang in there a couple more years until we graduate from high school. Two years seems to be an awfully long time when you are watching each hour of every day tick by, and now every hour of the night. I really feel betrayed by my dad. I thought I could count on him at least sometimes, yet he is obviously as afraid of mother when she's drunk as I am. Wow, what a coward. I guess I am too because I

I am lying here listening for any sound, afraid to close my eyes. She has come after me so many times before but this time she seems really provoked. Maybe she'll just pass out and sleep all night. I'll try to go to sleep now, if You will please watch over me, God. Hopefully it will all be blown over in the morning. I love you. Please wrap your loving arms around me and keep me safe until morning. Please God, be my eyes and ears.

Dear God, it's Me....Again,

Guess what? Mother is in the hospital again. She's been bowling with a new friend every Thursday night for a while now. Her name is Susie. They meet for dinner and drinks and then go bowling. There they drink beers all through the games. I know this because I had to go with her a few times. Often they would go back to Susie's house after bowling. I started babysitting on Thursday so I wouldn't have to go anymore. There was another woman who hung around with mother.. Her name was Carol. They had met when they were volunteering with our girl scout troop. This was during one of her happier stages. She can be very upbeat and active. She really seems to care about us in these times. Anyway, they ended up almost every afternoon drinking and watching a soap opera entitled, "Dark Shadows". All of her drinking friends seemed a little scary to me. I would always feel uneasy around them. Well, tonight mother wrapped our car around a telephone pole, and she has severe injuries. She has a couple of broken bones and her whole body is scratched and sore. She'll be in the hospital for a few days. God, do you think this might help her to stop drinking? I won't get my hopes up, but I don't want to give up on her. I don't understand why she has to drink so much to have fun? This incident is certainly not fun. I think she tries to stop drinking , but then after a while, she needs a new drinking buddy, and the cycle starts again. I can't remember them all. Sometimes the family will stay in our lives for a while. I think maybe they were trying to help our mother and even us. When she does come home from the hospital, we will do our best to help keep her smiling by helping her with whatever she needs. Maybe this time she will not have to go to a resting home.

Dear God, it's Me....Again,

It was a sunny day on a Saturday. We usually clean every Saturday. I was cleaning in the kitchen, and Miriam was sweeping the living room and dining room. Scott was outside getting ready to mow the lawn. Mother had not been down for her coffee yet. I heard this awful screaming from the garage. I ran outside to see my brother running through the yard with his pants aflame. I screamed for him to stop- drop and roll. Miriam was calling nine-one-one. I ran to the stairs and yelled for my mother. My dad was still working at the hardware store on the weekends. When the paramedics and the fireman got there, most of the flames were out but his jeans had melted into his skin. He ended up having third degree burns on both of his legs. He had to undergo several skin graphs and operations before he was all through. I pictured that incident for years. Poor Scott, not only did he still have to have a few more surgeries from his cleft palate and now this. What a horrible day this Saturday turned out to be! Thank You, God. I don't know what else to say

Dear God, it's Me....Again,

Today I was at college and then went to my shoe sales job at a local department store until about 9:30p.m.. When we arrived home, I heard my mother screaming at my father. Not that unusual. They were talking about the next door neighbors. Apparently they accused my brother of setting fire to the curtains in their living room. Mother had trouble with neighbors in every house we lived in. She would get mad, drink heavily, and then start screaming at them for whatever reason. These neighbors had two small children. There was a girl of about four and a boy about seven. Scott was still in junior high school but often played with them and rode bikes with them. The police had been called about the fire.. The firefighters put out the flames and the police investigated. Mother was livid! She ranted and raved to anyone who tried to talk to her. I found out later that the neighbor's decided not to press charges. I assume it was because they were afraid of what mother might do. These neighbors soon had a " For Sale" sign in their yard. They never spoke another word to anyone in our family. It was very sad. My parents did have to take my brother to a child psychologist for a few months. At our previous house, she had also ranted and raved with our neighbors. She said one of their boys had hit my brother in the face. She was always protecting him because of all the surgeries. The doctor, who lived next door, tried to explain to her that it was an accident, but she wouldn't even listen to him. She was threatening him that she would call the police. It just seems wherever we live, she's going to mess it up. Sorry for complaining, God.

Dear God, it's Me....Again,

Hey God, you are going to get a kick out of this. My sister and I watched the movie," The Exorcist" about a week ago. It was very scary. Since we share a car, we usually come home from working at the department stores between nine and ten at night. We would always take bets to see if mother was going to be in a good mood or a bad mood. They drink in their bedroom every night. My dad would come downstairs to make another "high ball" several times during the evening. Since we came home late, they were well on their way to a" buzz". We went up to the top of the stairs to their bedroom. The television was always blaring. We would reluctantly walk in and give them a kiss good night. We would take turns being the first one in. We could always tell if it was going to be a good night or a bad night, if mother had a scowl on her face. She would yell at us for one thing or another. If she was absorbed in the television, we would be relieved. So tonight as we were coming up the stairs, my sister whispered that this was just like in the movie," The exorcist".

Every time her Mom went upstairs to check on her daughter, she never knew which personality would appear. We both were giggling. From then on that was our little joke. My sister and I often made jokes to each other about situations like this. It was one of the coping mechanisms that helped us get through. We would roll our eyes at each other, we would cry until we turned it into laughter, and we would pretend that we really didn't live here. We make up scenarios about where we did live. I am so glad dear God, that you always make sure we have each other. I just thought you would like the," Exorcist reference". Good night God. I love you.

Dear God, it's Me....Again,

My dad has called us to the hospital. It's mother again. I wish I had a dollar for every time she has been in and out over the years. I could quit my job and pay for the rest of my college with no problems. Now that we are getting older, they tend to make up more creative excuses for her stays. This time daddy met us in the lobby after we had both gotten off of our evening jobs. He said that the doctors were suspecting heart problems. He said that she had probably had a heart attack and would need to stay for lots of tests and to rest. We went with Daddy up to the room to see her. She was lying there in a confused and dazed state. She told us she would be all right and they would get her heart all better. I caught my sister's eye. I knew we were thinking the same thing. Why were there no monitors hooked to her? Why was she not on an IV? She had no more had a heart attack than You or I. It was probably another suicide attempt. She had done this on a regular basis all of our lives. I'm in no position to try and guess if these were cries for help, accidental mixing of pills with alcohol, or just feeble attempts at attention. All I know is this puts the ones I can remember in the double digits. They must think we are really stupid not to put this picture together each time. I'm sure it was much easier when we were little, to blame things on outside sources but now? We both kissed her and said goodbye. Daddy left for the night too. He had driven himself. On the way home my sister and I talked about several of the other times she had overdosed. It made us sad for her that she's so miserable, but she keeps doing this to herself and to our family. Dear God, I'm praying that this time she can get help. Her pattern in the past is to change doctors each time they start to see she has a problem with alcohol. She seems to know just what to tell people so that she is not held accountable for her actions. Could you please help her to try this time? I know I'm maybe asking for the impossible since you did give us free will for making decisions. So far all her decisions have led right back to the bottle. Thank you, God, at least, for having us not be home this time, it was one less painful memory.

Dear God, it's Me....Again,

My sister and I have just received our high school diplomas. Our parents had always told us they would get us through college. We found out today that there was no money. They squandered and drank it away. Daddy still has his government job. He makes decent money. He could have saved some. I guess in the back of my mind I always knew that going away to school was wishful thinking. Miriam and I had both been saving our money to be able to move out. During high school, we babysat, we watched all the children in our surrounding neighborhood and we cleaned houses for a few of my mother's friends. I think it was You, God, that helped us with that. I think those friends knew something about our home situation. Now we only have enough to get us through the first quarter at the local university, so we each got a part-time job at Department stores. Miriam's was at Sears and mine was at Elder-Beerman's,where we worked to save up enough for each quarter. The bad part is, we cannot afford to move out. Our parents did pay for our books for the first quarter. We continued with all these jobs to be able to pay for classes, one quarter at a time. Also, Daddy kept "borrowing" money from us occasionally to pay for the electricity or whatever. At least with school and working we are not home much. We still make most of the meals and do a majority of the cleaning. My parents did buy us an old Chevy from one of the father's for whom we babysat.. Somehow we figured out the logistics to get each of us, where we needed to be sharing that car.. Finally, at the end of our junior year, we had saved up enough money to move out our senior year at Wright State University. We moved out, into a small apartment. It was so amazing! I slept so well knowing that there was no more fighting and screaming in the next room. No more violence. I stopped rocking in my bed. I was able to relax sometimes. At the same time Mother is going to school to get her RN degree that she started when she was a young girl. I hope this is Your way of giving her some direction. I do trust in the plan. You have gotten me through all these years. Thanks again for the diploma and the opportunity to still make my dream come true of being a teacher. I know these things I have gone through will help me to be a more compassionate person and teacher.

At this point we knew where we were headed. Miriam would graduate with a Bachelor of Arts in Social Work, and I would have a Bachelor of Science in Education. Our perseverance is paying off. We both know this would not have been possible without Your Mighty hand guiding us all the way. Thank you, God.

Dear God, it's Me....Again,

As you know, I graduated from college last May. I am the proud owner of a Bachelor of Science degree in Education. My sister got married in August and went to live with her husband, who is stationed in Germany. Her wedding was so beautiful. We made the wedding dress, and the bridesmaids dresses, ourselves. She got married in Philadelphia, where her husband's family lives. My mom threw a fit and caused a big scene at the rehearsal because the organist would not play, " Here comes the Bride ", as Miriam came down the aisle. Their Church teachings believe that the bride and groom come down the aisle together as they are presenting themselves as a couple who are joining in the Covenant of marriage. Then at the reception, which was outdoors in a beautiful setting of flowers and food hosted by the sister of the groom, there was a commotion. Miriam had come downstairs in her honeymoon clothes. They were headed for their new life in Germany. My mother and father were three sheets to the wind. Miriam said goodbye and she got into the car. Mother came running out chasing down the car as it pulled out of the driveway. She was screaming and crying that Miriam didn't kiss her goodbye. They saw and heard her but they did not stop. As we were all cleaning up that evening, there was my dad gathering up all the alcohol bottles. He was taking all full bottles and all that had anything left in them. I was mortified! Daddy said they had paid for it and, by golly, they were taking everything that was left. The booze was their only contribution to the wedding! I am so glad that Miriam was able to move away from mother. I was very sad that we will be so far away from each other. Thank You for Your grace, God.

Dear God, it's Me....Again,

B arry and I are on our way to Germany to visit Miriam and her husband. We will be staying almost two weeks! I have been so busy these last few months. We were getting ready for both weddings. Then I started teaching. Then having my wedding. It is the summer after my first year of teaching was under my belt. Now we are almost there! We will stay with them in their small apartment except for a few days when the two of us, Barry and I, are going on an adventure. We will take a bus to Paris and stay there two nights, then go to Lucerne, Switzerland to ride a cable car to the top of one of the Alps. The last leg of the journey we will be going to a Bacchus festival in Germany! We will have a great time. Please give us safe travels. Then when we get back to Wiesbaden, the four of us are going to a German beer festival. I am a little queasy being that this is my first time on an airplane. You are so good to me, God. We both love adventure and it is going to be great to be with Miriam. Thank You for letting these good things happen to me. I love You, my gracious God.

Dear God, it's Me.....Again,

I have landed a teaching position with one of the schools where I had been a student teacher. I am so excited! I am so happy to be helping others. My wedding was in October, soon after the school year had started. Again I made all the bridesmaid dresses and altered my sister's dress for myself. I was so glad that Miriam could fly home for my wedding. I have missed her terribly. My in-laws were wonderful. My parents were not. Too much drinking, too much perceived lack of attention for my mother, and too much drama. Miriam kept my Mom and Dad out of the way to minimize the drama. Luckily, You surrounded me with great friends and other family members that really cared about me. They were all too familiar with my parents' antics. What a whirlwind these last few months have been. Help me to just live every day forward, with Your love and understanding.

Dear God, it's Me....Again,

After our marriage, Barry and I settled into our jobs and enjoyed being together. Barry had graduated at the same time as myself. He was a manager at a local Garden center. He loved his job. I also love my job. I am truly doing what You called me to do. I thank You relentlessly. We got along so well. We went camping in a second hand pop up trailer. We love being outside in Your amazing world. We bought a sailfish and went sailing in the summertime. We went to Barry's family home every Sunday afternoon after I got home from church. Sometimes we would watch football or play games outside. I loved every minute of having a family that was so much more normal than mine. After about four and a half years we started talking about having a baby. I know it sounds like I'm living a Pollyanna life, but I was still dealing with my parents weekly from Texas. I also would become depressed and withdrawn. I would cry at the drop of a hat. I was taking medications to help with my depression and therapy to understand why. Every time we talked about change, I would get panicky. I know it wasn't easy on Barry. I was making bad decisions. I almost had an affair but didn't go through with it. A baby would be a huge change! Obviously, I love children, but I was terrified I wouldn't be a good mother. Look at the example I had. The pregnancy was complicated. I had preeclampsia and almost died at the delivery. So we pulled together to welcome our new child. Our sweet Natalie was born on July 15th 1982. Thank You, God, for being with us every step of the way. When Natalie was born with her cleft lip and palate, I felt like maybe You had let this happen to punish me. So I told Barry about almost having an affair. He was understandably very hurt and angry. I asked for us to go to couples therapy. We went every week for months. We did all our homework assignments, we communicated more, and talked about the effect of my family and our marriage. Then at a session, Barry said it was meaningless to keep coming. It was all about me and my insecurities from the way I was raised. I knew he was right. We tried for the next two and a half years. Natalie was facing several surgeries and doctor appointments. We both were working full time jobs. Spring was hard on both of us. It was Barry's busiest season and mine also with so many activities at school. We decided to separate to figure things out. Our divorce was final in July. We also agreed on shared custody. She would stay with me during the week and then go to her dad's house on Tuesdays and every other weekend. It was a very hard time in our lives. Guide us ,God.

Dear God, it's Me....Again,

My parents are moving to Texas. I can hardly believe it! I am helping them pack boxes and getting things together for the moving van. My dad has severe rheumatoid arthritis . His Doctor said the warmer climate would really help with his pain. He works at Wright Patterson Air Force Base in Dayton and was able to get a transfer to a base in Texas to finish off his last few years until retirement. Not only are they going to a warmer climate, but is almost two thousand miles away. I am still taking that in. Mother has a friend in Dallas that recommended A real estate agent to help them find a house in San Antonio. They flew down a couple of times to Texas and they have decided upon a ranch home in a suburb of San Antonio called Leon Valley. This will take a huge burden off of me in my day to day living. Mother could start a whole new life in Texas If she chooses to. God, I ask you to please watch over them in this new place. Mother did say they would join a church to help them make some friends. I wish they would make friends with You. They have decided to take Scott with them as he had no direction in his life. This is probably not the best for my brother but he plans to enlist in the Air Force as soon as he can. I know there will still be drama, fights and chaos in their lives. I will still get calls, letters and tears from my mother. On the other hand, I will be able to relax more and sleep better with them so far away.

Twenty Years with Mother in Texas

No Matter what the trials we face,
We trust in God to give us grace,
The ups and downs of day to day,
Will make us strong in our own way.

The good things keep us going,
The bad things hold us back,
But God will not forsake us,
He will always have our backs.

We learn from every situation.
To be gentle and be strong,
To ask for help, to seek the truth,
To show us right from wrong.

Dear God, it's Me....Again,

My mom and dad left for Texas today. I'm asking You to watch over them with safe travel. I genuinely hope it can be a new start for them. If the warm, dry air helps my dad with his rheumatoid arthritis, it could give him some relief. Speaking of relief, I felt a wave of emotion as they pulled away. Relief that I wouldn't have to be going to their house all the time. I also felt the weight of their presence lift up my shoulders. I didn't know what it would feel like to not always be at their beck and call. I know we will still be in touch but not on an everyday basis. I am 24 years old and I feel my teaching career is going well. I really love it. I'm teaching 7th graders math and science. My marriage to Barry is going well. We seem to be getting along and going on a lot of adventures. I do miss my sister as she is in Germany with her husband who's in the air force. My brother went with my parents to Texas to finish his last two years of high school. He plans to enlist in the Air Force as soon as he graduates. He also wants to get out from under the constant pressure and worry. I know You will watch over all of them. I usually dread big changes in my life because I don't know what is coming so it's hard to prepare. This time I feel like I can just pray that You guide us all and keep us safe.

Dear God, it's Me....Again,

Lord, here I am again asking for your help. I know you must get tired of hearing from me. I don't know what to do. I gave birth to a baby girl two days ago. She is healthy and strong but she was born with a cleft lip and palate. I know what that is because my brother was born with one also. I thought it was because my mother drank during her pregnancy. I didn't drink. I'm scared, confused and weak. I'll need your help to get me through this. I'm grateful that my daughter's otherwise very healthy. She weighs 8 lbs 10 oz. She looks so big in the Intensive Care Unit next to all those tiny babies struggling for their lives. Thank you God, for helping me choose such a good pediatrician. He is taking over and sent for a periodontist who's fitting Natalie with a retainer to keep her mouth from collapsing. They say this will save her several surgeries as she gets older. I feel like you are working here in my life because I don't have the strength. I am indebted to You. They had to take me down for emergency surgery yesterday. Part of my placenta was still in the uterus and was causing me to bleed excessively. I didn't quite know what was going on, but they kept putting ice packs on me all night, and at one point I thought I was over the bed watching them work on me. I was floating on the ceiling and looking at myself in the bed. I know my blood pressure dropped extremely low. There were six people working on me. I wasn't scared for myself, but knew I was going to have to be there for Natalie. Oh yes, I finally got to eat food today! Someone was supposed to have started me on real food right after the surgery. I was coming back from being in the sitz bath today. I was so weak I collapsed. A kind nurse helped me back into bed and ordered a meal. Thank you God for always being there for me.

Dear God, it's Me....Again,

I am so afraid. They just took my little girl into the operating room. She looks so tiny on that gurney holding her, "blankie". It is the silky summer robe that I wore the summer she was born. She loves to rub the material between her fingers as we rock and eat. I've given up wearing it and she even takes it to bed with her. Anything that gives her comfort. I can always get another robe. When I look down into that face with those big brown eyes, I think of my own mother. How could she want to leave Scott and have breakdowns, rather than holding him and loving his sweet face, reassuring him that everything would be all right. Maybe she just didn't know any better. I know we have to do this to repair the roof of her mouth. It's been very hard to feed her these past 10 weeks. We have had to use a syringe with a rubber tube attached to its end to squirt formula down her throat. Without a complete roof, her mouth cannot suck. I had been so looking forward to breastfeeding but that was not possible. I know getting her milk through this syringe is the reason for her being so colicky all the time. She was swallowing so much air. This does not seem to stop her from growing by leaps and bounds. She is so healthy in every other way. You know I have been glad to watch her grow and flourish. Please help her come through this operation all right. Please guide the surgeon's hands as they work on her little mouth. We will have to stay in the hospital for a week to ten days. I will be able to stay with her and sleep on a chair that folds down next to her bed. I was staying the whole time since her father is having trouble with all this. He's very supportive but he hates hospitals. He likes to be in control of a situation as you know. We are both in uncharted waters. I know who is really in charge, You are God. I put Natalie in your loving arms. The staff here at Children's Hospital is wonderful. I can see You working through many of them. I just hope she won't remember all the pain when she's grown up. I do understand that this is the first of several operations she will have to have. I just don't think we will ever get used to this pressure and worry. Her father and I are praying. That's where I'm counting on You, God, to get me through. Please, Lord, make these minutes stop crawling by like hours. Hallelujah there comes the surgeon. He is smiling. All has gone well! Thank you, God!

Dear God, it's Me....Again,

Wow, where does the time go? HerevI am again in the hospital and my sweet baby, Natalie is eleven months old. They just wheeled her away from her father and myself. She is still clinging to that raggedy old, "blankie". Please help this operation be as successful as the last one. Yes, it was hard to keep her from crying and teaching her how to drink from a bottle with an extra soft nipple with a large hole cut in the end. She can suck a little but still not like a regular baby. It really is so much easier than the syringe. She seems so much more relaxed too since she is a little more in charge. She has to wear braces on her arms to keep her hands out of her mouth. The periodontist made a device for her to wear from her second day on earth. This will help her roof from collapsing and it will save her several more surgeries. I am very excited about this operation to bring the two separate pieces of her lip together. When I see that face the next time, it will be without the gaping hole. I have tried to be patient with other people, but they don't know what to say when they can't say, "What a beautiful baby!". Of course I think she is beautiful because You have given me a mother's eyes to see her through. Please guide those working on her today. Steady their hands and open their hearts to take care of our precious child. We will be in the hospital again for five or ten days. You know how I love those fold out chairs that make a bed. The doctor has explained about the splints she will have to keep on her arms for about four or five weeks so she can't put her hands in her mouth while she is healing. She is not going to like that. As You know, she is already a head-strong young lady. I am so blessed to know how much You love and care for me and my child. I know with Your help, we will get through this too. I thought at first that maybe my daughter was born with this as some kind of punishment for me not being a good enough person. I have since come to realize that You will always be there for me. We will do this together.

Dear God, it's Me....Again,

I can't believe this is happening. I am getting a divorce. How did I let this happen? Why do I have to be so miserable? I know I have brought most of this on myself. I just can't seem to love people enough. I don't know how. I was never taught how. I am so afraid to give on that deepest level. It is so much safer to keep things light and on the surface. I can flirt, I can make friends, I can listen well to others, but I can't let go enough to really share myself. I know it is so much my fault. I thought marriage counseling would work. We have been going now for several months. He is stubborn and I am so weak. I know things have not been good for a while, but we have invested eight and a half years in this marriage. We have a four-year-old daughter together. We have been through so much with her. Shouldn't that have made our marriage stronger? I know I cannot go on like this. I have lost twenty five pounds in the last few months. I try to eat, but I can't. I have tried to make our marriage work. I am just not happy. I am sorry to be so angry. You are the only one I can truly get angry with without being scared like I used to be. I have seen and felt what anger can do to your flesh and your soul. I am going to go ahead with this divorce. You alone have the power to change things. I am only guessing this is what I should do. I have never thought I would get a divorce. My goodness, my parents are still together after hating each other after 30 plus years! God, help me as I try raising this child mostly on my own. We are moving into an apartment. There will be lots of changes. I don't know if I can make it on a teacher's salary. I am counting on You to help me through this as You have helped me through so much in the past. I could not even face this without knowing You are there. I have thought about ending it all but then I look into my daughter's sweet cherub face and know that that is not an option. How could my mother have ever considered this.? Hold me up, Lord. I'm so afraid.

Dear God, it's Me....Again,

As usual, You have sent me another way to help me cope. I am in this wonderful group of people who help each other deal with alcoholics in their lives. There are people in all walks of life in this amazing organization. The name is Al-Anon. These groups meet anonymously to give strength, hope and comfort to anyone who has been affected by someone else's drinking. The beauty of this is that we don't focus on alcoholics, but on ways we can change our emotional attachment to them. It is a time for people to share things that they have learned. That helps us to look at how our own behaviors can often escalate the situations we find ourselves in. We look at our reactions and feelings that come up. We learn how to keep calmer, say less in the situation, and keep our emotions from getting out of hand. I have found it so informative to give me tools to use. I know it is not easy. I'm reaching the end of my first year of meetings. I want to thank you God, for bringing my attention to this amazing group that helps so many people. I am not sure how long I will keep going to meetings but I will keep using and learning from these suggestions and examples as long as I need to. God, thank You for reminding me that I'm never too old to learn new things. All my love to You, God.

Dear God, it's Me....Again,

Thank you for empowering me tonight. Mother called again in the middle of the night. She and daddy were fighting again. She was crying and pleading with me to help her. She was slurring her words as she usually does, wanting someone to save her. What could I do from so far away? They had moved to Texas a few years ago for Daddy's health. Here I am in Ohio. He has rheumatoid arthritis really badly and the dryer climate seemed to help his pain. They had restarted their pattern of violence in the middle of the night. They would both be drunk and start in on each other. They would scream, throw things at each other and physically fight. It has escalated since my brother, the only one of us still at home these last few years, had enlisted in the Air Force. One of them would call me and ask me to talk to the other one to calm them down or just to listen to the injustice of it all. I have my own family now and a full-time job. I cannot keep answering these calls and still get up in the morning. What was happening was that I would stay on the phone until things calmed down. Both of them would be passed out within the hour, and there I would be wide awake and worried for the rest of the night. All right, let's just get through this. Tonight when mother called. She was sobbing so hard I could not understand much. She said she had locked herself in the bedroom and Daddy was trying to get in to kill her. I told her to call the police but she refused. I told her I would call them and send them to her house. She said no that she didn't want to get Daddy in trouble. I was furious! She was expecting me to believe she was in fear of her life, but wouldn't call the police?. Something snapped in me tonight. God, I'm sure you are the one to finally open my eyes. I cannot and should not have to deal with this 2,000 miles away. I told mother, calmly, that I was going to hang up and call the police and that she was on her own. It was a simple step but I always felt I had to be dragged into the drama to be a good daughter. Tomorrow when they are sober, I will tell them I will not be answering the phone after eleven o'clock.

Dear God, it's Me.....Again,

Well, when You set out to create a new beginning, You don't mess around! Not only will my divorce be final this week, but I got the new job at the school much closer to home. This will cut my travel time in half and give me extra time with my daughter everyday. It's a little unnerving to start at a new school after nine years. It feels like a clean break with the past. I feel You are allowing me to start my life fresh. I will not disappoint You. I know that teaching is the gift You gave me. I am able to be there for those children that need someone to care and listen, much like the teacher You put in my life so many years ago. You have taught me that the subject matter is inconsequential compared to the compassion involved in a classroom environment. The best part is that my daughter will be able to attend this school too. I will be able to be with her and care for her. What more could a single mother ask? I think back to the summers we were sent here and there. Why wouldn't a mother want to be with her children? Only You, God, could have orchestrated this so beautifully. I am again humbled at your awesomeness. Help me to be a success and to serve You well. What a week! I had better get busy looking over that Junior High science curriculum so I can start out on the right foot. Thank You again for your guidance and love.

Dear God, it's Me....Again,

What in Your name am I doing? Have you let me go insane? I am getting married today! I was never even going to look at a man again. I have been making it on my own. My daughter and I have done better than I expected. I've learned so much about myself and the things I need. I'm growing closer to You everyday. Thank you for seeing me through. Thank you too, for helping me to find Al-Anon. It has given me such insight into how I grew up and how my heart has been shaped, hardened, torn, softened and healed. What a wonderful twelve step program. It has helped me make new friends, look at my shortcomings, and get closer to You. I never thought I could have enough confidence in myself to try marriage again. I know there are no guarantees in anything, but I will try not to fail You this time. I know that I really did not fail, I really did the best I could with what I had. I am not the same person who stood before You and made those promises the last time. I am more open to love. I have felt the true promise of hope You have given me..Please know that I do not make this commitment lightly. You have been the one constant in my life since those early days of the closet altar. You have strengthened my relationship between a mother and her daughter. I have learned to put pieces of myself out there that had never seen daylight. I feel You have led me in this direction. I know I can do this. Please know that I do not make this commitment lightly. You've been the one constant in my life since those early days of the closet altar. I will try not to disappoint You. This time I will give it my all, just as You have been giving me your all. You have led me to a man who is caring and intuitive. He has given me the gift of accepting me for who I am. This makes me want to work even harder and become the person You want me to be. Help us continue to grow together in good times and in bad. I know Alan is taking on a huge commitment to help raise a small child. Give us both the patience we will need. Thank You too, for allowing my sister to be here to support me.

Dear God, it's Me....Again,

My parents are coming from Texas to pay us a visit. They were not able to travel when I married Alan, as my mother had had open heart surgery. We've been married for almost a year. They bought a huge recreational vehicle from the money her mother, my grandmother, had left for her when she passed away. They will be here tomorrow. They are going to park it in our driveway. They are going to hook it up to our house through our basement window. Not sure what they're going to do with their waste. Alan isn't really looking forward to meeting them. My mother "fell" walking outside and tripped off the curb; She broke both of her legs a few weeks ago. That is the story they told us. So, she will be arriving on crutches. Of course, they are bringing their dogs. One is a golden retriever, and one is a black lab. I can't wait for the fun to begin... not. Sorry I should not be sarcastic. I do want Alan to meet them. They called yesterday to say that they took out a mailbox on their first day of travel. They did not stop. She thought it was so funny. My stomach has been turning all day. They will be staying with us for about a week. They will visit some old friends,and do some catching up with them. I just hope everything will go smoothly. I had forgotten the tension I feel whenever I'm around them. I will breathe deeply, smile often and, try to enjoy the time with them. I have seven years of Alanon under my belt. So that should help. I am not going to believe that I am not good enough ever again. Well, I will just hope for the best and ask that You give me strength and patience. I love you, God.

Dear God, it's Me....Again,

I am lying here in my bed putting my heart in Your hands. Today, at my job as a counselor, it was one of the worst of my life. I have been working with a girl for two years, whose father drinks too much and is very mean to her. We have talked a lot about how alcohol can make people do things they really don't mean to. I have tried to get her to share with me but she is so protective of him. I can relate to her because of how I grew up. I always felt, if only I could be a better daughter, or complain less, or do more around the house it could keep things from turning ugly. I realized she was trying to do the same and yet she needed some kind of attention so badly that even negative attention was better than none. She's been acting out lately and when she gets in trouble at school, I strongly suspect she is getting abused at home. Well, today she came into my office and was willing to share with me. Her father had been drunk, gotten mad and pulled a wooden board from his carpentry supplies and beat her. She admitted that it was finally time to share the truth with someone and try to get her dad some help. She said this had been going on for years. Her mother had left when she was a baby and she had no one to protect her at home. When she showed the bruises to the authorities and myself it took my breath away. Her little bottom was one huge blue and purple mess!. It brought up so many feelings for me. The first was anger at what this man had done to this sweet innocent girl. Then anger at what alcohol can do in a defenseless child's life. I was also angry at my past that I too had had to deal with this kind of abuse. I too always wanted protection. I feel like I could handle it myself and with my sister's help, rather than to blame my parents. It hit me right square in the eye that alcohol or not, no child should ever have to live with this kind of pain and fear. She went to live with her aunt today, while there is an investigation. I'm praying now with all my heart that her dad can change his ways with help and that she never has to go back to living in that kind of environment. I now understand how much you protected me and I'm asking that you protect all children in this situation until they can have the courage to speak up and get someone to listen.

Dear God, it's Me....Again,

I was sitting in the backyard enjoying the warm spring weather You have sent. I heard this weak little cry. I looked around but didn't see anything. Then I heard it again. I got up and went toward the sound. There under one of my tomato plants was the most beautiful cat I had ever seen. She is a long hair Siamese seal point with bright blue eyes. She appeared to be less than a year old. Not still a kitten, but very young. She just kept meowing and talking to me. I got her some food and water and she lapped them up. She let me pick her up easily. As I ran my hand down her back I felt a large bump. It appeared to be a piece of metal embedded into her neck. She also had an open gash on one of her front paws. My compassion took over. Here was one of your precious creatures asking me for help. I could not turn away. I took her to the vet and they did emergency surgery. Someone had shot her with a bullet. The vet said she probably had been abused in other ways too. I immediately felt the connection. I just couldn't believe someone would not be missing her though.

I put ads in the paper and checked with the local shelters but no one seemed to want this beautiful cat. She has fully recovered and has been an answer to my prayers as You know. I love cats but my new husband was sure he was allergic because he has sinus problems. I thought I would never be able to have a cat. Here you sent her to me. Alan fell in love with her as much as I did and now she is such a great part of our family. To me she represents the abuse and harm that I went through. Here's my way of feeling some of that. I give back to her some of the total unconditional love she gives to me. Her name is Sammi. If only the whole world could treat each other like this. I call her my little piece of heaven. Her purr is loud and confident and she senses whenever I am upset. Thank You for sending us a precious gift in my garden of tomatoes.

Dear God, it's Me....Again,

How can I ever thank You for today. As You know, Alan and I recently bought a house. It is a very scary thing to do. We just wanted a place of our own. I didn't want to raise my daughter in an apartment atmosphere. I am trying to redo my budget. I realized that we had more debt than I thought between Alan and myself. I decided to try to find a consolidation loan today. I went to five different banks and was turned down. One bank said they wouldn't because we had only just gotten married. Another bank said that because I had just started a new job, that they wouldn't be able to lend me the money either. The other three Banks had very similar things to say, even though I had always paid my bills on time. Too many changes in a short time to be stable enough. I was crying all the way home. I was so disappointed. As I was driving home, I saw a Citizens Federal Bank. That was the bank I had my checking account with. I suddenly got the urge to turn to them for one last try. I think subconsciously, I hadn't tried there because it was a small local bank. I wiped away my tears and went in with my head up high. A manager agreed to see me. I laid out what I needed to show her and explained that the consolidation loan would help me pay off higher interest credit cards. She was so nice. We talked for over an hour. She decided to take a chance on me. When I was getting back in my car, a weight lifted off my shoulders, and I immediately realized what You had just done for me. I am forever grateful for how You step in and answer prayers that I haven't even asked You for yet! I am humbled.

Dear God, it's Me....Again,

What the heck do You have me doing now? Here I am about to walk out in front of hundreds of people I don't know, in a bathing suit. I have been going to therapy to try and understand myself and the way I grew up. I am starting to feel better about the person I am. I've been working on my self-esteem. There are so many mixed messages from the past I'm trying to sort out. One of the assignments was to do something I had never done before that would push me out of my comfort zone. I started taking modeling classes. One thing has led to another. I've gotten a few modeling jobs around local Department stores. I was even in a bridal show. Now, somehow, I was talked into entering a Mrs. Ohio contest. I never dreamed they would accept me. I still often feel like that fat ugly girl with braces. I'm over 30 years old! When I got the letter, I was shocked. I had to get sponsors and pictures and now I am here in Columbus with twenty-five other ladies in a beauty contest. Wow, what a leap from the girl who hid in the bathroom in high school so people wouldn't look at me. I'm trying to learn that I am beautiful inside and out because You created me that way. It has not been an easy task. I have a lot of old tapes and messages playing in my head from the past. I look in the mirror and I'm not sure I see what everyone else sees. This is what I'm trying to accomplish. So here I stand ready to walk out on this stage. I will hold my head up high and keep a smile on my face.

Dear God, it's Me....Again,

Well There goes Natalie again being wheeled off to the operating room. At nine years old, she no longer needs her "blankie", but I sure still need You! The last three times in the hospital were just short overnight stays. She has had two pairs of ear tubes since her sinuses don't drain, and she's prone to ear infections. This is another big one. You would think it would get easier to stay calm and not worry, but I still feel that uproar in the pit of my stomach and the clatter in my brain. I've asked this before, so You know what is coming, please guide the hands that are working on my daughter today. This time there are two surgeons. One will take a bone graft from her hip, and the other will attach that bone into her upper gum. They say it will grow into place and help make up for the bone gap she has from the cleft palate. I'm so glad You have sent us such skilled professionals. Later they may be able to actually attach a tooth to that bone in order to perfect her smile. Of course I think she has the most beautiful smile already. She's been wearing braces on her teeth for the past two years. She will have to wear them again later, after all this heals. It is so amazing what You have taught me to do. It was so hard to see her fear this time. She's old enough to have an idea of what is happening. I was able to calm her, the way You always call me. It did help when You sent her a whole Girl Scout Troop to visit her last night! Please continue to create serenity for our minds and fill our hearts with Your love.

Dear God, it's Me....Again,

Here I am calling on You again, God. I'm sitting here in this graduate class wondering what I am doing. I haven't been in a classroom as a student for over sixteen years! I have been a teacher. I'm going to have to make myself vulnerable again. I hope I can do it. With the new state standards for continuing education, I knew I wanted to be working toward a goal. I prayed to You about the course of action I should take, and this is the direction You led me. I'm going to someday become a school counselor. Of course I had to choose a major with seventy-two credit hours. It is going to take me a long time taking one course at a time, but here goes. I have to start somewhere. Please help me to not make a fool of myself. At least there are a few older people in this class. I was afraid that everyone would be twenty-two and I would stick out like a sore thumb. I'm very excited and apprehensive at the same time. There's that old knot in my stomach, but at least this time I have caused it to be there, and not uncontrollable circumstances. I'm always so glad I don't have to do anything alone. You are always by my side.

Dear God, it's Me....Again,

Here I am calling on You for strength once again. I just got devastating news from the surgeon. I have breast cancer. I felt the lump a couple of weeks ago. I tried to put it out of my mind. I went in for the mammogram last week. I was fairly confident because I had my first mammogram fourteen months ago and it was all clear. This time the technician kept coming back to take more pictures. She took ten in all. My heart was sinking with each one. My stomach became knotted and my breath shallow. Sure enough, I had two tumors. Three days ago I went for a stereotactic biopsy. I have to admit I was terrified. I had to lay on a table while they inserted a needle into the tissue of my breast to get a sample of the tumors through hollow needles. Okay, they found two. It was a long and tedious process and it was not a pleasant experience. It wasn't supposed to be that bad, but I guess the base of the tumor was so deep they had to dig a little. I had to lay perfectly still while they did an ultrasound to know where to stick the needle into each tumor to draw out some of the tissue. They'd given me a local anesthetic, but I guess it was deeper than they thought. I was trying to lay still but I was shaking from head to toe. I saw the mammogram and the ultrasound pictures. The main tumor was about the size of a tennis ball with tentacles reaching in all directions. They say that is not good. Right now I am in a daze. I'm going to have to put myself in Your hands. I have no idea what else to do. I don't understand why this is happening. Do I still need to learn patience? I just have to believe in Your plan. I know medicine has come a long way in the past few years. We will be scheduling the surgery for next week. It seems like it is happening so fast and yet each hour is torturously long. I will be in the hospital for about a week. The only other surgery I've ever had was my tonsils out at age five. They are offering me reconstruction of the breast. They will be taking out the breast during the mastectomy. They want to take tissue from my tummy to rebuild a new breast. It's a good thing You gave me so much extra fat there. I will no longer have any feeling in that breast, but at least it will fill up my bra. I will have to take five weeks off from school. I hate to do that to my students, but I know You will watch over them too. Please give me the strength that I will need to get through these next few weeks with strength for my family. I still have a lot I want to do. I'm only forty-two. They have told me that if all the margins are clear and there is no cancer in my lymph nodes that I will not need chemotherapy. I thank You with all my heart for that. I'm counting on you God, I can't do this on my own

Dear God, it's Me....Again,

What is happening? Tell me I'm having a bad Nightmare and I will just wake up soon. My husband went to the doctor with a sore throat, but he has not been able to get rid of it for the past two months. His doctor put him on several antibiotics to clear it up but he kept having a constant tickle and sore throat. She sent him to a specialist to check his throat. He said it was probably nothing so I didn't even go with him to the appointment. Then he came home and told me that they did a needle biopsy on his tonsils. A biopsy is to check for cancer. I know that all too well. God, please no... I have already gone through this and I wouldn't wish this on my worst enemy, much less the man that I love. I'm trying to keep positive, yet it has only been two years since my treatment. I am so scared for him. I know he has to be scared too. He has seen what it can be like first-hand. We are sitting here waiting for the call. He never was a smoker. He hardly ever drinks. He's in good shape and takes good care of himself. He works out regularly and has a third degree black belt in taekwondo. This is not the kind of person who gets cancer. I know that everything happens for a reason and that we can only see such a small piece of how we fit into the universal picture, but if there's any way this could be prevented, I am begging you dear, God. The phone just rang. It is cancer. We hold each other and cry. You have shown us that cancer can be beaten. With Your help we will get through this too.

Dear God, it's Me....Again,

I'm sitting here on the porch swing watching my husband riding the lawn mower to do the yard. He loves to work outdoors and he has made our landscape a beautiful sight to behold. As I watch him, I know he is tired. He's been having radiation to his throat, five days a week for the last six weeks. He's had to take off work because he has so little energy. His job is very labor-intensive and requires a lot of walking, standing and lifting. Ironically, the lack of energy is not from the radiation itself so much, as to the fact that he cannot eat. It hurts to swallow anything and he has been on a totally liquid diet for the past four weeks. He's been taking those nutrient supplements and having to use that "magic" mouthwash to try and heal the sores in his throat from the radiation. He has lost over thirty pounds. He's taking it all so wonderfully. He has a great attitude. He jokes that he needed to lose weight anyway. He never complains and still wants to do what he can around the house. I've mowed a few times and I do the hand mower around the edges of the yard. There he is, exhausted, hurting and hungry,. doing one of the things he loves best: working in the yard. God, you have shown me so many people with strength throughout my life and my trials. He is definitely one of them. I'm so sorry my husband has to go through this process. I would not want anyone to have to go through cancer and its treatments, much less in such a difficult way. You have given me a new perspective on living and enjoying each day. I pray to You that that will be one of the good things to come out of this situation for him. Also,. please help Alan to get through this and be healed. We have a lot to do yet together and growing old with each other is one of those things. I hope the next couple of weeks of the radiation will be smooth, but most of all help them to be successful.

Dear God, it's Me....Again,

Thank You SO much for seeing Alan through his cancer battle. He finished up eight weeks of radiation and four weeks of healing time. Now the doctor says it is all gone. Hallelujah! He will have to go for checkups every two months for the next 3 years, but they say these first few months are the most critical. The doctor also told him that if he had not followed through when he did, with the persistent sore throat, that it probably would have killed him. Tonsil cancer is one of the fastest growing cancers, and if untreated can spread very fast. I know that had to be Your work, God, because Alan is not one to usually go to the doctor. They have had to do three more surgeries to get all clean margins. They had to take out a part of his tongue. He will need a few more weeks of recovery before he'll have his strength built up enough to return to work. His taste will never be the same. Some of it will come back but not all of it. Alan cannot taste sweets anymore. After the first bite they taste salty. The doctor said he would probably stay about this weight for the rest of his life. That is a small sacrifice to pay for getting your life back. I just wish there were more impressive words to say to You besides" thank you". I just don't seem to be strong enough. I rededicate my life to spreading Your love and miracles to everyone I can. Alan is back to work and slowly getting his energy back. He has also put on a few pounds. He has had to have speech therapy and voice therapy. He has been so positive! You sent me an amazing man. We now know, with Your help, we can make it through anything.

Dear God, it's Me....Again,

I want to tell you how grateful I am that You called me to be the youth director of our church seven years ago. A couple of years before this, the previous Pastor asked me to do this. I was teaching Sunday School classes at the time. Natalie was little, and I was working full time and my husband at that time, thought it would be too much. I agreed reluctantly. A few years later when my daughter was 11, I was asked again. Although I was still working full-time and taking classes for my masters in school counseling, the time seemed right. I always try to answer when You call. I made the decision to lead the youth group with a mission influence. Of course over the years we had a lot of fun outings such as lock-ins, Super Bowl parties, and ice cream socials. We had many activities as fundraisers for our annual summer mission trips. We would have car washes,we sold candles and made cookies in a jar or anything else we could think of. The participation in each event earned the kids points toward their trip. When we got close to our goal, each young person had to fill in their price gap by getting sponsors. Each mission trip was in a different part of the Eastern United states. We went on these in the summer. We went to Ocala, Florida, West Virginia, Michigan etc. We joined hundreds of other youth from around the country. They would assign each small group to do things like painting a shut-ins house, building a retaining wall, planting a garden just to name a few. There was a praise service every night. We got half of Wednesday off to explore and share what each other had been doing. We did all this in Your name. I am thanking you God, for guiding us. We also went each year to an amazing weekend of Christian music and worship. It was at Asbury College in Lexington, Kentucky. It was called Icthus. We could always see little miracles and testimonials. You filled our hearts. I bring all this up because after seven years I am stepping down. My breast cancer has returned a second time and so with all the radiation, chemo and surgeries etc. I won't have the energy I need. I have loved every minute of serving You in this way! As I say good night, it is with happy tears in my eyes. I am grateful for the opportunities to serve others, the bonds I have made with youth, and helping us all come closer to You. I love You!

Dear God, it's Me....Again,

Oh God, please wake me from this nightmare! I can't believe I'm going through this again. Why? The chances of cancer coming back in a reconstructed breast are minuscule and yet, it has happened to me. I was so happy these last two and a half years since the surgery. All the margins were clear, no lymph nodes involved. They said I did not need to go through chemo or radiation. My odds were fantastic to have gotten it all with the surgery. I've worked so hard these last two years to finish my master's degree in school counseling. I've started this new phase of my life with such renewed faith and determination to make the most of every day. I love my new job. My daughter is in college, my life is so good. You wouldn't take that all away from me now, would You? I know I just have to slow down and have faith. You got me through this once. We can do it again. When I noticed that hardness in the reconstructed breast, they said it was probably just scar tissue since it was right along one of the suture lines. When I noticed it was getting bigger, I had a gut feeling. I just came from the surgeon's office. Thank You for making sure a good friend went with me. They did the biopsy right there. Sure enough, cancer again. A different kind this time. Oh great, I am one in a million. With those odds, why couldn't I have just won the lottery? I will put my life in your hands. There is nothing else to do. I do have to admit that I am scared. The feeling in the pit of my stomach is starting to feel permanent. I now have to go through another mastectomy, radiation and chemotherapy. I have asked everyone I know to put me on their prayer list. Your servants are strong and the collective faith of many will get me through. Please calm my fears so that I can be a strong example to those around me. They are still trying to decide the best order for treatment. I guess I'm the talk of the cancer seminar in town. I'm going to get through this. I don't believe You have brought me this far, through so much, for this to be the end. I know you have more plans for me, as I do for myself. I love you dear Father, calm my spirit.

Dear God, it's Me....Again,

O h my God... please help me. I am so sick. This was my first round of chemo. They gave me something called, "The Red Devil", adriamycin-cytoxan. I can't seem to stop throwing up. They gave me something to help with the nausea, but it doesn't seem to be working. I went in this morning and they took my blood to see if I was good to start. They hook me up to an IV and then drip this stuff into my arm. I have good veins, so I may not have to have a port put into my skin. A port is a device that they put surgically into your chest so that they can put in medicines without having to search your veins each time. A port has been known to have lots of complications, so thank You for that little bit of good news that I won't need it. We'll just have to see how it goes. There was something in the IV to help me relax and feel kind of sleepy. It took about 4 hours to get it all in. There were about eight of us in the room all lined up in recliners with IV's hooked to our arms. Wow, if they do this everyday with different people for 3 weeks, until our time comes around again, that's a lot of people with cancer. It's almost too mind-boggling to comprehend. When my IV was empty they let me go home. I thought I was going to just sleep the rest of the day until this nausea started. Now here I am hugging the commode and retching my insides out. I know I have to do this. I know with Your help, I can. My friend's daughter, who is then went through this and I saw how strong You made her. She's my hero. I tutored her all during her treatments for leukemia. She was so brave through it all. She had treatments for over a year. If she can do it then I can do it then so can I. I will have four rounds each three weeks apart. Then we'll have surgery to remove the reconstructed breasts. Then eight weeks of radiation and finally another four rounds of chemo. It's too much to think about now. I think I'll call the doctor and ask if there's something else I can take to help with the nausea. I put my life in Your hands.

Dear God, it's Me....Again,

Well, they said it would be somewhere between two and three weeks when my hair would start to fall out. Here it is day seventeen and it is coming out in large handfuls. I have long dark hair a little past my shoulders. Or should I say " had". I knew it was coming and one of the Angels You put in my life, gave me a gift certificate for a wig. I took my 19 year old daughter with me the day I went shopping to get it. We tried several on. We laughed about creating a new identity and going blonde. We experimented with long, short, curly and straight. In the end we settled on a wig very similar to my own hair color and style. I work with small children and I didn't want the difference to be too drastic for them. If I could help it, I was only planning to miss two days, every 3 weeks when I got the chemo. They wouldn't even have to know I lost my hair. Now here I am today standing over the sink pulling out my tresses. I knew it was coming but you are never really prepared for the moment you see yourself with just small clumps here and there. My dear husband has offered to do the honor of shaving off what is left. He kindly and gently lathered my head and went to work with a razor. I'm not sobbing and crying like I expected. I just have quiet tears rolling down my cheeks as the hair falls onto the ground. It really is a small price to pay to be able to see your daughter graduate from college and continue to live a life geared to helping others. Thank You God, for the Angels around me to help me through this. Today, Alan was my Angel.

Dear God, it's Me....Again,

This is my fourth round of chemo. It hasn't been too bad since the first one. You are so good to me. The new nausea medicine they gave me does wonders. As long as I lay in bed and sleep for the first 24 hours after the IV. I'm doing great. I still have to go in every week and get my blood counts done to make sure I'm tolerating the toxins. I now have to get daily procreate shots to boost my red blood cells and help give me energy. I get so tired so easily. I also get something for the white blood cells so they will keep fighting off infections. This chemo does quite a number on the immune system. I had to go to the hospital the other day and sit in the emergency room for three hours because I ran a temperature of 102. They had to give me IV antibiotics but luckily, I didn't have to stay overnight. This is the most exhausted I have ever felt in my life. I'm glad this will be the last round before the surgery. I have complete trust in You that it is doing all it is supposed to do. When we met in the chemo room today, we had a good time. There are a few of us who always get our treatments and shots on Wednesdays. One of the ladies always brings a joke to share. One lady brings her Bible and reads us her favorite scripture from the week. We will join hands around the room, many times to give You thanks and praise, as well as to pray for each other and our families. These are more of the angels that you send to help me get through these times. I am eternally grateful for your grace. Thank You for helping me to get through each day. Please, dear God, let this chemotherapy work.

Dear God, it's Me....Again,

I am about four weeks into my radiation treatments, as You know. There was a three-week break between chemo and the radiation. I was doing very well. It was a little bit of a hassle to go to the hospital every day after work, strip down to the gown and go to the radiation room. The whole process only takes about 45 minutes. Today I was talking to a teacher in my office when I had to excuse myself from the conversation to go throw up. This was very unusual. I guess I'm not feeling too well. I went to the restroom and looked at my chest, which had been hurting. My skin had turned completely black! No wonder it hurts. I had noticed getting redder each time I went to radiation but it had only recently become uncomfortable. I went to my principal and told him I might have to go home. It finally occurred to me that the pain was causing me to vomit. He had also had a bout with cancer earlier in his life. He said we should go to the hospital right away. I just wanted to go home. He said he would drive but we'd have to take my car. He didn't want me to throw up in his new Lexus. We drove down to the hospital. He demanded the doctor see me. Thank You for his assertiveness. At that point I did not have the strength to be assertive. When they saw my skin they immediately put me on antibiotics and gave me a special cream to put on my chest. Sometimes the radiation effects can accumulate into a dangerous burn. Thank You for placing people around me who can often do for me what I cannot do for myself. They gave me a week off of the radiation schedule for my skin to heal before they had me finish my last four weeks of treatments. Thank You for not letting that happen again. Once was enough for me. All I can say is, I hope the radiation is doing its job. Sometimes I feel like the cure is worse than the disease!

Dear God, it's Me....Again,

Oh dear God, I am so tired. This is the last round of chemo. I did 12 weeks before the surgery, Had the surgery and then did eight weeks of daily radiation. This is the end of another 12 weeks of chemo. Thank You so much for having the timing work so well. This last round of treatment was during my summer break from school. I don't know if I would have had the strength to work every day, like I did the first time. I was so proud of only taking a few days away from school then. My body is really crying out to me. I ache all the time in my arms and legs. They say this is a side effect. I've had to have medication to boost both my red and white blood cell count. I can do a few things and then my energy rent just runs out. It's like I hit a wall and can't move another inch. I've lost most of my taste for food and I have these sores all over the inside of my mouth and tongue. I have to gargle and drink the special concoction called," magic mouthwash" that helps with that. Just like Alan had to have. The steroids I'm taking are keeping me bloated and hungry even though nothing tastes good. It's sort of ironic, the one time I could probably lose weight easily and they don't want me to. I am asking You today to make sure all this is doing what it's supposed to. I am tired and discouraged and depressed. I know that I can live with all these feelings to have a life free from cancer. It's just that sometimes my faith in You and this whole process wanes but only for a moment. Please send me a boost of spirit. I'm lying here on the bed petting my cat Sammi. She's been with me every day all day. It is as though she senses that I'm not well. She purrs and snuggles with me. I've started calling her," my little piece of heaven" because she keeps reminding me how much You love me and would never forsake me. Help me to keep taking one day at a time and to look for the small positive things each day. For example, yesterday You sent my friend Paula over with a movie. That was so sweet. I had to tease her because she fell asleep during the movie. She had been working so hard. Just the fact that she thought of me and came to spend time with me helped me through yesterday. My little Sammi is helping me through today. I'm trusting in You lord. I believe You have me in the palm of your hand. If I could just be a little less tired.

Dear God, it's Me....Again,

I just got back from Hospice today. I stopped after church to visit her. She was in the cancer support group we started with our chemo room buddies. There were six of us originally in the group. We would meet every other week to pray and go over scripture. It gave us all peace and the feeling of Hope to read your word. We read stories about those who have suffered and been healed. We would bring in music with inspirational lyrics and sing the songs together. We would lay hands on each other and pray for our individual aches and pains. We would deal with our tumor markers and our prognoses. We met together for over 4 years. The group would grow and ebb as people would come and share their stories. Nancy, our main leader, would bring in speakers to tell us about nutrition and eating as it related to cancer. We read books and articles together to learn more about the causes of cancer and the latest research. Nancy was our inspiration. Actually, she would say, we all inspired each other. When the first member of our original group passed away we all had a special memorial service and shared stories of her courage and attitude. Today, Nancy passed away. We are all going to her funeral together and to the graveside service.. We never met formally again after that but some of us keep in touch by phone. It just didn't seem right without Nancy. She was such a child of Yours ,sharing hope, faith and understanding. Today at hospice, I learned another member of our group has now come to be with You also.. I'm not sure why you have chosen me to stay here and be healed, but I thank You and praise You. Please guide me in your will as I want to make the most of this time You have granted to me here on earth. I do not always understand You God but I love You and trust in You completely.

Dear God, it's Me....Again,

It has been a crazy year. Alan had to go back to surgery three times until the Doctor could finally find clear margins. This last surgery they even had to take a part of his tongue. He then had to do speech therapy, voice therapy and constant checkups. The poor man has lost a lot of his tastes. Sweets turn salty .Many things are bland. The doctor says this may go partly away over time. He has a hard time chewing and swallowing. I usually have to make a sauce or gravy to help food slide down his throat. He also has to take smaller bites. He has been through so much. He is keeping a great attitude. Please, dear God, Help him to get better everyday. He is starting to slowly get a little weight back too. Alan is back to work now but taking it easy. He is getting his stamina back a little every day. He is a proud man. He hardly complains at all. I am eternally grateful for You putting him in my life. We still hold hands and tell each other we love them. I know with all my heart that You are watching over both of us. Thank You for always being there. I love You Lord.

Dear God, it's Me....Again,

My sister and I flew into San Antonio today. My dad is not doing so well. Of course, my mom isn't very good at taking care of him. It has been mostly the other way around all their lives. His arthritis has really gotten bad, and he has been diagnosed with Congestive Heart Failure. He's supposed to eat a healthy diet and get more exercise. Well, that is not working as neither of them cook very often. They eat out or get fast food almost every day. Since my dad retired, he is not moving around like he used to. They spend a great deal of time at home in their bedroom watching television and drinking. The doctor says he may have only a few months or even a few weeks left to live. Miriam got a plane ticket from Philadelphia with a layover in Cincinnati. I booked my flight from Cincinnati to Texas. We ended up being on the same flight to Texas. We spent the whole plane ride talking, reminiscing about the past and worrying about my dad and what would happen to my mom when he passed. When we landed, we were picked up at the airport by one of their church friends who drove us to my parents home. When we got there, both greeted us at the door. My dad looks so tired and worn out. Mother just burst into tears. We tried to console each of them. Someone had cleaned up the guest room and it looked nice. There was a pathway from the cluttered kitchen right through the living room into their bedroom. Their bedroom took me by surprise. I gasped as I saw newspapers and magazines and trash piled higher than the mattress on my mother's side of the bed. They filled up the whole space from the bed to the wall including the whole length of the bed. The ceiling fan obviously hadn't been used for a while since there was a 3 inch thick stack of dust rising toward the ceiling from each fan paddle. I could hardly breathe. There was a rush of anger and hatred when I saw how they were living. No wonder my dad was getting worse with every day that passed. I went to the bathroom, which someone had cleaned, wiped the tears from my face, and did some deep breathing. At least my sister and I were both there together. My sister took their car and went to the grocery store. I made myself busy in the kitchen clearing off some counter space and getting dishes into the dishwasher. We made a simple dinner and talked to them the rest of the evening catching up on our family and theirs. Miriam and I decided before we went to sleep,that tomorrow we would clean that bedroom. Dear God, here I am at your mercy. Please send each of us the courage, strength and stamina to get through tomorrow. Give us a good night's sleep for energy tomorrow. I love You, God I will let You know how it goes.

Dear God, it's Me....Again,

What a day dear God! Thank you so much for giving us stamina to push through today. It was a long day. I was getting through an hour at a time and sometimes a minute at a time. We filled at least ten bags full of trash out of that bedroom. Filth was overwhelming. Two or three times I had to go in the backyard to gag and cry. I didn't want my parents to see me. I'm still angry. Not just about this day but how for years we had lived in these similar conditions.. It was hard for me to breathe because of all the dust. If I couldn't breathe, no wonder my Dad's health has been going downhill. So, I would take a trash bag to the garage to get some fresh air like I did yesterday. We washed all their sheets in bed clothes and wiped down every inch of the shelves, the walls, and the floor. We would often find a random shirt or jewelry box mixed in with all the trash, so we had to filter through it. Not that mother would have missed them. How can you live like this? I felt the knot in my stomach growing bigger. When we finally finished, we both took turns taking a long shower and crying. It helped me to get some of the things I was feeling go down the drain with my tears. We took them out to dinner at a huge Texas Roadhouse that my parents wanted us to see. It was set up like an old fashioned Saloon and there was a girl on a swing over our heads. Talk about going from the sublime to the ridiculous. We will be leaving tomorrow to go back home. Mother insisted we all go to church so we can meet more of her friends. I'm grateful that these people have helped them in our absence. Please give us safe travel. Thank you, God.

Twenty Years of Mother Back in Ohio

Each Stage of life is different,
We find It's Ebb and Flow.
We use Our Wisdom and Our Strength,
Based on all that we know.

Some say it's like a roller coaster,
With ups and downs and turns;
And each new situation,
Uses what we all have learned.

We know not where our future ends,
Or when Our Days Are through;
But everyday is such a gift,
And we owe it all to You.

Dear God, it's Me....Again,

Miriam and I were called back to Texas. It was almost a year to the day since we were there to clean. My dad was in horrible shape. He was in the hospital with severe Congestive Heart Failure. The first day we were there, Hospice was called in. Mother was a total mess. This man she had been married to for forty-four years was dying. We went to the hospital each day with her. My sister and I took turns spending the night with Daddy. Miriam spent the first night at the hospital. I took my mother back home and made sure she got something to eat and drink. Of course she had to have a highball or two before she went to bed. I got my mother up the next morning and made sure she ate breakfast. We went over to the hospital. Daddy was getting worse. We talked to him and tried to reassure him but he knew. I stayed the first night with him. We were watching ice skating. He always liked a pretty girl. A respiratory therapist came in with a breathing treatment. Each breath was so painful for Daddy. I asked the therapist to not come back and to skip the next treatment since Daddy had been put on Hospice care. He said he hadn't heard from the doctor yet. After that attempt my dad was coughing and in so much pain. I talked to him for a while. He seemed to be in agony. I asked him if he could see a white light and he nodded yes. I told him to look for Angels and his mom. By this time it was early morning. I called Miriam and told them to come soon. He hung on until they got there. He was sleeping and his breath was shallow. They sent me home to get some rest. I got the call about an hour and a half later. He was gone. I think he was waiting to say goodbye to mother. Dear God, I know You welcomed him Home. I am so glad he is no longer in pain. We stayed for the funeral. It was sad.

Dear God, it's Me....Again,

I am asking You once again for patience and courage. As you know, my parents moved to Texas about 19 years ago. My dad had rheumatoid arthritis which kept him in a lot of pain. My dad worked at the Air Force base in Ohio. His doctor suggested a transfer to a warmer and drier climate. It really did ease his pain for many years. Well, my dad passed away about a year ago. Daddy was always my mother's main caretaker and chief enabler. With him gone, mother had no one to take care of her. She had a nice group of women from the church that helped her with the grieving process. I was here in Ohio, taking her drunken calls of misery as best as I could. Yesterday I got a call from one of her best friends. She told me they could no longer handle her. She told me I needed to move her back to Ohio. Mother had been drunk dialing her friends and acquaintances. The police were called on several occasions. Obviously, she had not been taking her bipolar medication and was drinking in excess. They promised to get her house sold and packed up. This was no easy task as she is a hoarder who doesn't clean. My sister and I had gone down for our dad's for funeral and had cleaned the worst rooms. I remember having to go outside a couple of times to throw up. The filth was disgusting. I flew her here to Ohio and we looked for houses she could afford. We found a nice small house (easier to clean), less than a half mile from my house. So, I am heading back to San Antonio next week to bring her home to her new house. That is why I am, once again, asking for the strength and courage to not only bring her here but ultimately to be her caretaker. Hopefully not her enabler. There is a fine line between those two things, especially with my mother.

Dear God, it's Me....Again,

Let me tell you about my last couple of days. I arrived in San Antonio just before 10:00 a.m. I stopped on my way to get coffee for my mother. The moving van company had loaded her belongings the previous day. She seemed in a pretty good mood when I got there. I think the coffee helped that. Most of her furniture was either on the moving van or sold. She had kept her bed in Texas to sleep on these last couple of nights. My husband and I had already purchased a new bed for her house in Kettering, Ohio. We had assembled it and made her bed with all new linens and covers. We had also gotten her a television and cable, all waiting for her to arrive. The house in Texas looked better than I thought it would. There was some leftover trash in some of the rooms, and several boxes left to hold her kitchen necessities that she would need until the moving van arrived in Ohio. I packed, and loaded, the full boxes into the car's truck. I also put the dog food, dog dishes and leashes in the car. Yes, we were taking her two large dogs on this 1000 miles plus journey.

We left Texas that afternoon about 3:00 p.m. We stopped at a fast food place to eat dinner and take care of the dogs. And we drove on to the motel that accepted pets. we got settled in and of course she had brought along some wine. The next day we set out on the longest leg of our journey. It is hot and long. I'm taking more breaks to walk the dogs and give them water. Mother is whining a lot. I have pasted a smile on my face, and we keep going. When we finally reached the dog friendly motel of the night. I got us unpacked and mother is lying down. I'm taking the dogs out for a walk. Brittney is a golden retriever. She's about ten and well-behaved. Pandora is a black setter, about three, not so well-behaved. There was a small wood behind the motel, so I'm taking them there to do their business. Pandora is pulling on the leash so hard she finally slips her collar. I take Brittany back to the hotel room. I set out to find Pandora. I'm calling her and walking deeper into the dark woods. I can't find her anywhere. I am crying now and that old feeling of knots in my stomach has surfaced again. Please God, help me. I don't know what to do. I searched some more and then headed back to our room. I was feeling desperate. I opened the door to see mother with her glass of wine staring at me. I'm trying to explain what was happening, when there was a bark at the door. Pandora had made her way back! She had probably followed Britney's scent. Thank you, God, so much. I'm going to bed. I'm exhausted. Tomorrow we will arrive in Kettering. The start of a new phase of my life.

Dear God, it's Me....Again,

Mother has been living in her house in Kettering for about six months. I helped her in the placement of her furniture in each room. She starts out helping me but then has to go lay down. I helped her organize her closets, drawers and kitchen. She has been very cooperative so far. She has met the neighbors. On the one side is a single mother with a small boy. On the other side of her house is a wonderful neighbor who is three years older than mother. Her name is Wanda. They have really hit it off. They talk almost every day. She has been taking mother to church on Sundays, a domino group on Thursdays and to the Woman's Club downtown twice a month. Wanda and mother both play the piano. They have a lot in common. I am so pleased, dear God. I know in my heart that You orchestrated this friendship. My mother was seventy years old when she came here from Texas. She comes to my church fairly often too. Mother is settling in well. Maybe this move will be a positive step for my mother. Love You, God.

Dear God, it's Me....Again,

I took my mother to a new doctor. He is a geriatric doctor who deals only with the older generation. It was a small miracle that You got her to agree. He is very nice. He was friendly with us. He was in his sixties and she was in her eighties. He really empathized with her. He talked directly to mother. He made her feel heard. I was there as a fact checker and a caring daughter. He asked her lots of questions. He gave her a written test, a physical test and a mental test. I gave him a list beforehand with all her medicines and diagnosed one of them being bi-polar. He let her ask as many questions as she wanted. He was so gentle with her. We agreed we would come back next month. He even gave my mother and I his personal phone number. The next day he called me and explained what he had seen. She had all the signs of Alzheimer's disease. He put mother on an Alzheimer's medication to hopefully slow the progression. I am so grateful dear God, that again, You have shown me I am never alone in this process or anywhere. I told him I was thinking about starting the process of becoming her guardian so that I would have help in getting her what she really needs. He told me it was a long process but that it would be a good idea, especially as her mind declines. The next month he told me he would send a report to the lawyer who was helping me to get guardianship,' Thank You', doesn't seem to be enough. I would be lost without You, Lord.

Dear God, it's Me....Again,

Today, I was just finishing a classroom guidance lesson, when the secretary called me to come to the office. When I got there, she handed me the phone. It was my mother's neighbor, Wanda. She was out of breath and almost hysterical. She told me to come quickly as my mother was chasing her around the house and in the backyard to get the bottle of wine that Wanda had taken away from her. My mother was in a rage. I ran the half block from where I work, to find mother still chasing Wanda, but in her underwear! Wanda forgot to mention that part. God, I'm not missing the irony that this is the house that You helped us find for her. It was almost a year later I was hired at that school, half a block away. The police were called, and they helped me get my mother dressed in her clothes. As we were wrestling with her, she was shouting profanity and even taking swings at the policeman. She landed a pretty good blow on his face. I was scratched up and assaulted also. When she goes into these rages, she is very hard to subdue. I kept talking to her in a calm voice. When the ambulance got there, my school was just letting out. Of course all the "walkers" were passing by us. I am the school counselor there. I met the ambulance at the hospital emergency room. They had given her medications to calm her down. I stayed with her as she slept through the effects of the sedative. They wanted to take her to the psychiatric floor, but she convinced them that she had been given a new prescription by her doctor and she was just reacting to that. She promised she would call her doctor when she got home. Of course this was a lie. She yelled at me all the way home from the hospital. In her mind, it was all my fault. She locked me out of the house for the next few days. I had a key to the front door but not to the storm door. I didn't push it. I really just wanted to make sure she was still alive. Thank you, God for keeping me calm, even though it was very embarrassing. Love you.

Dear God, it's Me....Again,

I got another call yesterday, this time there was a fire in my mother's kitchen. She left the plastic container that held plastic utensils on the stove and forgot to turn off the burner she had used. The plastic melted and gave off a ton of dark black smoke. Soon it was all through the house. When I got there, the firemen were still spraying the house down. The kitchen was demolished. The rest of the house was filled with black smoke and water. Mother was quite hysterical. Wanda and I tried our best to comfort her. I called the insurance company, and they were really cooperative. I gathered some clothes for her and put her in my car to take her to my house. She really wanted to stay at her house. As I tried to explain the situation and that it was dangerous for her to be in the house until it was cleared. She opened the car door and attempted to get out. I slammed on the brakes. She proceeded to start walking home. I followed her in the car begging her to get back in and go to my house. She was not having it. She walked the rest of the way with me following behind in the car. She promptly locked all the deadbolts so that I couldn't use my keys. Wanda came over and tried to reason with her. So, we just had to leave her there. The next day, Wanda, mother and I met with the insurance company and they were really cooperative. They could put her up in a hotel, or stay with me, or with Wanda. Mother was told it would take about a month until she could go back to her house. She refused to stay with me, so Wanda graciously offered her home. That was such a moment when I felt You step into our situation. They will pay $100 a day for room and board. Mother will be right next door to her house and keep her dog with her at Wanda's. Thank You God, for sending me an angel in Wanda.

Dear God, it's Me....Again,

Mother is back in her house! The company that came to fix her house was awesome. They gutted all the kitchen and we picked out new cabinets and new appliances. They painted every room after cleaning up all the smokey walls. They even gave her new carpet. I think, even mother, was pleased. It gave me a chance to reorganize her things. It was fun finding a place for each thing. The process took awhile as mother would get to a point where she couldn't make one more decision. She would scream at me to get out of her house. I kept coming back until we were through. She had lived here quite awhile since coming from Texas. The house had needed a good cleaning anyway. She just couldn't seem to ever put things in the right place. At least I didn't have to start from scratch this time.

Dear God, it's Me....Again,

Guess what, another late night call. This time it was from Wanda, Mother's friend, who lives next door. Apparently, mother had gotten into a quarrel with some people across the street earlier today. About what, I have no clue, but of course she got drunk as the evening passed. She decided to take a rake out of the garage and continue the argument. She used the handle to knock out the glass in their front window. It was after midnight, and it scared the neighbors to death! Mother was screaming profanity and waving the rake. Wanda had intervened and talked to the recipient of Mother's wrath. She explained that she was not in her right mind. By now I think the whole neighborhood knew of her escapades. I got there just as the police came. I explained about my mother's condition and told the neighbors that I would gladly pay for the window and its installation. They kindly refused to press charges. I was taking my mother to her house to put her to bed. Wanda asked if mother could spend the night in her guest room. I think it was so she could be sure she didn't go back outside again that night. I went home and tried to get some sleep. God, I just keep putting out fires that I didn't start. My sister and I have decided it may be time for some professional help. Please guide me in the right direction. I'm about at my wit's end. Love You and good night.

Dear God, it's Me....Again,

Today I got a call from the neighbor on the other side of my mother's house(not Wanda). There was a tree about six or seven years old in this neighbor's yard. A few of the branches were hanging over into my mother's yard. This neighbor has a ten year old boy. He was climbing the tree as most children like to do. Mother got her small chainsaw out of her shed and proceeded to cut off those branches, while the boy was still in the tree! The neighbor was a grown lady whom I used to babysit back in my teens. Again God, You put angels in my life. Luckily she did not press charges. Yes God, I removed the chainsaw to my house. I was embarrassed and angry. I can't seem to truly understand how she does these behaviors. I know a lot of this is because she doesn't take her medications on a regular basis. This is the fifth time she has attacked a neighbor in less than two years. I'm going to start looking for an outside agency that will come to her house a couple times a week. They could help keep her company, straighten her house a little, give her the medications and make a meal or two. I contacted the Area Agency on aging. They are sending me some places that they would recommend. I'm going to have to bring up the subject with mother. This could keep her in her house much longer. She came to live near me at the age of seventy. Now she is in her low eighties . The constant change in mood keeps me on high alert. I really hope this will give mother, and myself some sense of relief. Thank You, God.

Dear God, it's Me....Again,

Wanda and I have both refused to buy any more alcohol for mother.. The incidents are popping up almost regularly. She still has a car and she has been going to the store to get it herself. We have explained to her how dangerous this is. A few months later she went to Kroger to buy wine. She was leaving her parking space and backed into the lane to leave. She didn't look and almost hit a man. He was banging on her car trying to get her to stop. She sped away and put her car in the garage. Of course, the man reported her to the police. She had a vanity plate that said," Air Force Mom". The police were knocking on her door in no time. She refused to come to the door. They went next door and the neighbor gave them my phone number. I had given my phone number to several neighbors because of her bizarre behavior. This time I got a call at work. The police were asking me to come to my mom's house. I had a key. At first, she wouldn't unlock the deadbolt and kept screaming for us to go away. Finally, the policeman told her that if she didn't cooperate she would be under arrest. She tried to deny anything happened. The police cited her with a hit and run misdemeanor and gave her a court date. I of course, had to find a lawyer, take her to court, and pay court costs. That is also when I found out she had to let her driver's license expire as well as her car registration. This is when I took over ALL of her bills. I sit down with her once or twice a month to write the checks, after I rummage through drawers, cupboards, and under furniture to find the statements. I have bought her several baskets to put by the front door to put her bills. I've spent many hours practicing with her in my car so she could pass her driver's test. It was all to no avail. She failed three different driving tests. Each about three months apart. I secretly knew she would fail and she should not be driving in her condition. I was trying to have her see for herself and meanwhile leaving her some dignity.I felt as though I should let her try to do it on her own. After her third test, she realized she wasn't going to be able to do it. We sold her car about two months later, and that took care of that. Wanda, her friend, drove her to Columbus to get an official Ohio photo identification card. Wanda is such a kind and gentle soul. This is such a relief to me. One of my biggest fears was that she would hurt herself as well as someone else. Thank You, God, for putting a calming hand on my heart.

Dear God, it's Me.... Again,

Today I met with a lawyer who deals in Guardianship and Estate Planning. After all we have gone through, to keep mother in her home, it just isn't working out. He walked me through the process of becoming her guardian. What a process it is. I will have to take classes online to explain how this works and what kind of forms I need, how to fill them out, and how to document everything through the court system. I'm overwhelmed. It is going to be very time consuming. I know I must do this because I have tried so many other things. On some days she's apologetic as I'm searching through the trash trying to find her bills to pay. I refill all her prescriptions and put the right pills and dosages in the weekly meds box. Sometimes she will take them but mostly she will not. When I go there every week or more I must prepare myself for what I will be dealing with. Sometimes I'm treated like a daughter and other times I'm yelled at, degraded, and spit upon. I just try to keep an even voice level. I have come to realize just how little she is able to control her emotions. If I can't get her settled down, I just leave and try again the next day. My first task is to prove she is not capable of taking care of herself. I will have to file incompetent paperwork. Then we will go to court and present my reasons. A co-worker of mine said I should just declare her a ward of the state and be done. I just can't do that. She has some great comprehensive days. Well, I better get busy starting on my online learning. Please be with me, dear God. I can do all things with You beside me. Love You, God.

Dear God, it's Me....Again,

Well, I had another encounter with the police tonight. It was 1:30 a.m. Apparently mother was drunk again and took some clothes that Wanda had given her and dumped them on the Wanda's front porch. She was outside screaming and yelling, laughing and crying at the top of her lungs. Mother often throws fits when she doesn't get her way. I don't even know what triggered tonight. Wanda called me and I called the police. I told Wanda to not open her door for any reason. I wanted to make sure Wanda would not be in danger. I met the police at mother's door. She was inside still raging as we knocked and rang her doorbell. I didn't want to scare her, but I hoped the police would calm her down. I finally used my key and opened the door. The police were right behind me. She was still raging at me and she slapped me across the face. My glasses flew across the room. The policeman stepped in to try to calm mother down. They managed to subdue her. They said they were going to take her to the hospital to make sure she was all right. The one policeman retrieved my glasses and asked me if I was okay. He asked if I wanted to press charges. Of course, I said no. If only she could take her medications on a regular basis. The police took her to the hospital. I followed them there. After I made sure Wanda was okay. This sweet lady who had befriended my mother has gone through a lot. I felt so bad for her. She doesn't deserve this kind of treatment. Actually neither do I. When I got to the hospital, the police approached me again to see if I was all right. They decided to pump her stomach since we don't know how much alcohol she had consumed and if she had taken any or all medications. There had been many suicide attempts during her lifetime. I stayed with her the rest of the night. After talking to the doctors, they decided to put her on a seventy--hour psych hold.. This would enable them to adjust her medications. I went home anxious and upset. When will all this end? I got a few hours of sleep and then went to work. At least she will be safe for the next three days. Dear God, give me strength.

Dear God, it's Me.....Again,

Today I am meeting with the Guardian ad litem from the court, at my mother's house. Mother was served papers a couple of weeks ago, telling her that I was trying to get guardianship of her. She was so mad! I finally had to leave because she was screaming at me and trying to grab me. I'm so anxious about the meeting today. It is hard to tell what her reaction will be. I met the court lady in front of my mother's house. I had told Mother that we were coming. We knocked several times. The front door was locked so I finally used my key. As the door swung open there was mother coming out of her bedroom all disheveled and barely awake. I explained what the lady was here for. I introduced her to my mother. Her name was Alice. We all sat down. The lady was calm and gently explained what the process was about. Mother was seething. She was staring me down and not looking at our guest.. The lady asked a couple of questions. Then suddenly mother leapt out of her chair and came after me. I barely had time to stand up and back away from her. Alice got up and put herself between me and my mother. She explained to mother that she was just there wanting to meet her as part of the Court process. Mother sat down and so did I. Alice started asking my mother some questions. All of a sudden, mother was screaming at both of us. She was calling me an ungrateful daughter trying to take all of her things and yelling at us to get out of her house. She was screaming and cursing profanities. She called the lady a " nigger" and went after both of us. We both headed for the door. Mother slammed the door behind us and locked it. We could still hear her as we walked down the driveway. I was SO embarrassed! I kept apologizing to Alice for my mother's behavior. She asked me if my mother was going to hit me. I shook my head yes. I didn't tell her how often that had happened in my life. I couldn't stop the tears that were running down my face. She gave me a hug and walked to her car. I was exhausted but headed back to work. Thank You God, for being there with us.

Dear God, it's Me....Again,

Here we go again. I was just closing my eyes to sleep, when the phone rang. It's never a good sign when it rings after eleven pm. There was a man on the line telling me that he gotten a call from a woman who was almost incoherent and that she had taken some pills. He said she was trying to reach her friend by phone, but couldn't remember her friend's number to tell her goodbye. He said he asked her if she had any relatives close by and she gave him my number. He had her on his landline and he was calling me on his cell phone. I asked if he could try to keep her on the phone until I could get there. He agreed. I hung up immediately and called the police. I called Wanda, her friend next door and asked her to try and check on mother. I told Wanda I would be there in three minutes. The police and I arrived at mother's house in tandem. All her doors were locked and she had put on the deadbolt so Wanda had not been able to get in. I unlocked the door and found her slurring her words into the phone. That kind man had kept this perfect stranger on the line until we got there. I thanked him and got his information. I am sure, dear God, that You had something to do with this situation. She reeked of alcohol, and sleeping pills were strewn all over her bed. Just about then the ambulance arrived. They were loading her up and they asked me to meet them at the hospital. When I arrived they were pumping her stomach and putting charcoal down her throat to soak up the toxins from the pills and alcohol. I stayed well into the night until she was given the all clear. They did keep her on a seventy-two hour hold because of the suicide attempt. I eventually arrived home in time to grab three hours of sleep before I left for work. I suddenly realized that you,God, had saved her life by using that nice man as an angel to intervene. What a miracle! This was far from mothers first attempt at suicide. There were many throughout her lifetime. She is always able to get help in time. She obviously has other mental health problems. I sent the man on the phone flowers the next day. Thank You, Lord. I love You.

Dear God, it's Me.... Again,

Today I brought three friends over to help me clean up mother's house. She is somewhat of a hoarder. I have been trying to keep it somewhat uncluttered with the help of Alan and Wanda. If we try to do anything while she is there, she just gets mad and kicks us out or starts accusing us of taking her things for ourselves. Wanda has taken her out to lunch and dominos. This will give us some time. I made my friends promise that they would accept payment or they couldn't help. It is just so embarrassing. We each took a room to start. One was in the kitchen, one in the living room, and two in her bedroom. Her bedroom was her main living space. Clothes were strewn everywhere. We couldn't distinguish if they were dirty or clean. The small dresser next to her bed was overflowing with papers, cans and bottles, candy wrappers and of course, wine glasses. Filling up the entire space under her bed was more of the same. We put things into piles. . Clothes, underwear, important papers, miscellaneous items, and trash. Oh, so much trash. We cleaned the counters in the kitchen. We threw out all the spoiled food and rot from the refrigerator. I gagged as I cleaned the bathroom. I wouldn't let any of my friends do that. Alan and I had just cleaned a couple of months ago. I don't know how one person can create this much of a mess. After all of us had been working for three and a half hours, it was looking pretty good. I paid all my friends and after we all got cleaned up I met them for lunch. We all had to take a shower. The next week I started with a home helper agency that would come twice a week. We went through a few people before we found one that mother liked. Often mother would not let them in or send them home. I am doing her bills twice a month now. I have her sign her checks , so she feels like she is responsible. I still must look under her bed and in her drawers, to find most of the bills. I had put a basket right by the front door just for bills, but they often didn't make it there. Please bless my three friends who were able to help today. God, please keep sending me strength and courage to get through each day.

Dear God, it's Me....Again,

Today I am meeting my lawyer at the courthouse. I have taken all the on-line classes, filled out all of the paperwork, copied all the documents, crossed my "T's and dotted my "I"s. I believe I am ready. I did not want to have to do this but could not find an easier way. I asked my mother if she wanted to come with me to court a few weeks ago. At first she was all about coming and letting them know what a horrible person I was. She was going to get her own lawyer and sue me. I offered to pick her up for today's hearing, but she refused to come. I believe her friend Wanda helped her realize that I had to do this for mother's safety. I doubt mother agreed with that but decided not to pursue it. I was SO anxious sitting outside the courtroom with my lawyer, waiting to be called into the proceeding. I felt that knot twisting in my stomach and throat. I felt terrified to do this. It feels like I am that small child cowering in my bed awaiting for what would happen next . We were called into the courtroom. The judge went through my paperwork. The statement from the geriatric doctor, the forms with all her assets listed, the history of her diseases and the guardian Ad Litem report from Carol were all there. I was so embarrassed by Carol's report as she listed everything that had taken place that day, but that that was her job. I shrunk down in my seat as the judge read the part of what mother called Carol. It was a horrific name. It was all there, and they gave me guardianship of my mother. It was finished. Now would come the hard part. I will need to slowly convince my mother to move into assisted living. God, I am counting on your guidance, counting on my friends and counting on my family. This will be a long, steady walk over these next months and days. I love You God.

Dear God, it's Me....Again,

The first girl from the agency started last week. so far so good. She is very friendly and easy to talk to. Mother was fighting this process, but I kept reminding her that this could keep her in her house. We're going to start out on Mondays and Thursdays. She will be there 3 hours a day. Well, the first week went pretty well. I came from work to meet Sue at the door and let her in. We talked about expectations and taking mother's meds every day she was there. We all three were getting along fine. She cleaned the kitchen and put days worth of dirty dishes in the dishwasher and then put them away after it was finished. She spent a lot of time talking to mother and getting to know her. I left after an hour and went back to work. The second week Sue started picking clothes up from the floor and hanging them up. My mother would start to get agitated, she would stop. She would make some coffee. Mother loves coffee, and just started up a conversation. I was starting to breathe more normally. Well, this Thursday, the last day of the second week, mother did not answer the door. Sue called me and I came with my key. She was sound asleep at 11:00 a.m. There were wine glasses all throughout the bedroom. I explained to Sue about mother's swift changes in her moods. She wanted to stay and made a pot of coffee for my mother. I left to go back to work. It was the first little glitch in our plan. I know You are helping me, God. Hopefully Sue is willing to stick it out for a while.

Dear God, it's Me....Again,

So, it turns out that Sue was the head of the company that comes to help Mother on Mondays and Thursdays. Sue has been coming now for 3 months. She had a new girl she brought in last week. They both stayed for four hours on Monday. It went well. On Thursday, this new girl that had been there on Monday came to the house by herself. I have a call at work two hours into her time. She said mother was not happy with her. She reported that mother was being very mean and inappropriate. She had been cursing and calling her names, so she was leaving. She was black. Mother's filter has been degrading over the past few years. I apologized to this girl and assured her that I would pay her for the whole four hours. Well, this week the agency sent me a new person, so I met her in front of my mother's house. I'd explain to mother that she really needed to be cordial to these people who are coming to help her out. She was named Anna. Anna came on Mondays and Thursdays. It was going well. Maybe this Anna will stay a while. I got to my mother's house. I go to my mother's house every Wednesday and we usually go out to dinner. I check on her medicines and clean up what I can. The helpers have really taken some of the strain off my shoulders. I really hope this will work out. Wanda has also been helping by buying organizers and helping mother to better know where her things are. Wanda also takes mother to a domino group that she frequents. Thank you, God, for sending me so many of your angels. it truly does take a village. Thank You for helping me through all these changes to help Mother stay in her home.

Dear God, it's Me....Again,

Well, I have gone through two more agencies and it is always the same story. This last agency sent a new girl in. Mother seemed to get along with her. After another month, Teri asked if I could just pay her directly and she would help mother go through her house and help mother decide what she wanted to take to assisted living. Over the last year things have been up and down. When a mother is depressed, she is much harder to work with. She started locking her door and not answering the doorbell. I remind her that these caregivers are here to help her. They are coming to the house, she says fine, but then tells them she doesn't need them today. It has been hard to find helpers who want to work with her. Also, I cannot keep paying people who she won't let in. I talked to her and encouraged her to work with these people who want to help her make her life easier. This is the third agency that we have tried. I'm afraid that living in her house alone will not be an option for much longer. The house has become worse since the last agency left. I do what I can when I'm there doing her bills, when I am refilling her prescriptions, filling up her weekly pill containers and cleaning dog poop out of the carpet. She won't let her dog out if she doesn't want to get out of bed. This comfort helper is named Teri.. She is middle-aged and is just down to earth. She tells mother what her goal is for the day and somehow gets mother to help her. When mother is whining about something, she just tells her that this is the goal we have for today. just as a matter of fact, as if they were old friends. I'm really impressed with how she handles mother. I'm trying to remain positive, but my mother's health has been worsening over these past couple of years. Her geriatric physician has been tracking her health and memory. Teri has some good days with mother. I've explained how hard it has been. I asked her if she could start thinking about downsizing. Mother is aware that I think she needs to be in a safer environment. She fights me on it, but I do think she may feel deep down, that the day will come. Teri has been coming now for about 10 weeks. She has led mother through her closets and drawers. They are weeding out what mother can't wear or doesn't need. Teri and mother both know that I have recently become her guardian. I feel so many emotions. I'm sad it has come to this. I am angry that all the things we have tried have only been Band-Aids in the long run. I am sad mother doesn't have the things she wants. Miriam came in from Philadelphia and she and I went to many assisted living places. Some won't keep her after she runs out of money. Others wouldn't let her bring her little dog. We took mother to our top three picks. She hated them all. So Miriam and I picked the best one. We have started the ball rolling. God, please help us through this next phase.

Dear God, it's Me....Again,

I am really going to need you tomorrow! We are moving my mom into assisted living. We have set up a plan that we all hope will make it easier for everyone. My sister is coming from Philadelphia to help Teri and I, mostly Teri, have been going through mothers belongings with her to make sure she will be surrounded by some of her favorite things. We have a truck and a U-Haul team of people to get her residence set up. Alan and I will be in that group. There's another group that will move things in and set up her bedroom, bathroom and living room. My sister, Miriam, will be with them. Wanda will be taking mother to lunch and a movie so that mother will be less anxious and upset. She knows this is coming. We have discussed it with her many times. In many ways. She has yelled, screamed, cussed, and gotten violent. We've run the whole gamut of emotions. I keep stressing that this will help her have better care and keep her medicines regulated. I know she hates the idea. Thank You so much for sending me such a great team of friends and family to help get this finished. I can imagine that she feels betrayed and hates me doing this to her. I wish a part of her would know that I'm not doing this TO her but FOR her. I feel we have tried everything to avoid this. The assisted living facility is clean, friendly, doesn't smell, and caters to the residences needs. My sister and I searched high and low to find the right place. Some are beautiful as long as you keep paying them. When you run out of money and have to go on Medicaid, they won't let you stay. Others have just a room, others have suites. This one we picked has a little apartment, even a small kitchen. There was a back porch with french doors in her bedroom to let her dog out. Yes, this is one of the places that allowed animals. I'm trying not to stress out. Mother asked what I would do if she refused to go. With tears in my eyes, I said I would have to call the sheriff. Please be with all of us tomorrow as we put this plan in motion. I love You God!

Dear God, it's Me....Again,

I come to You exhausted. What a day! As soon as Wanda and mother left for lunch, we all got busy. We loaded up all the things mother had chosen to take to her new place. My team loaded it all and then unloaded it at the assisted living facility. The team there went to work arranging everything in the living room, bedroom, bathroom and kitchen. They organized all her closets, pantry and bookshelves. They were working on that while we took the U-Haul back and threw away as much trash as we could out of the house. I'll be working in the house for the next couple of months. We need to start getting her house ready for sale. The cost of the facility is more than she receives from Social Security and my dad's pension, so selling her house will be key to having her needs met for a few years. I can't thank You enough for giving me the help of such good friends. We couldn't have done this without them. Miriam and I decided on this plan to keep the stress level of our mother to a minimum. She wouldn't have to make quick decisions about how to arrange furniture and belongings. Of course, after she gets settled, she can arrange things more to her liking. I'm hoping that mother can make some friends and get settled in enough to feel content. if they give her medication to her regularly, she could actually enjoy living there. Wanda and I will each visit at least every week. I will take her out to dinner and or take her to Wanda's house. It will be a lot, but I will have the peace of mind to know that she is eating and taking her medications. I know it will be an adjustment for all of us, but she was becoming a threat to herself and others. Thank You, my dear sweet God.

Dear God, it's Me....Again,

I have been working at my mother's house since she moved to assisted living at the end of April. Thank You so much for helping me get my mother's house ready to sell. I worked for hours almost every day since school let out in May. The first day I went in and sat on the living room floor. I looked all around and I was just overwhelmed at the idea of the task. I just sat there and cried for about 20 minutes. I was angry and frustrated. Then I called my sister in Philadelphia. She talked with me, and we cried together. Then she reminded me of something we learned in Al-Anon, just start somewhere that seems doable. Just concentrate on that area until it's finished. I started in the living room closet. I pulled everything out and made four piles: trash, donate, garage sale and whatever is left over. I started to go back to my steady breathing. I've been having panic attacks for some time. We had gotten our mother settled in an apartment at the assisted living facility. I had to sell her house so we could pay for her new living situation. I worked every workday for four or five hours all through June. I gave myself the weekends off to keep my sanity. My husband and I filled his Ford F-150 ten times with trash to go to the dumpster. Alan was so patient and helpful dealing with all this, and with me. I did have friends come by to help when they could. One of the reasons it was so much work was that I would have to go through piles of papers and trash by hand because there might be a deed to the house, jewelry or letters mixed in with everything. It was a daunting task. We would have the garage sale the last weekend in June. Alan and I set up empty boxes in the garage. We put old doors across the top to make shelves. That is where we will spread out all her dishware, knick-knacks and anything breakable. We would put anything we didn't sell into the empty boxes to go to charity. I had finished with the house cleaning, had the carpets cleaned and sorted again for the garage sale. I had some good friends who helped put things on tables in the garage. We put all the books, records,and organizers in the yard, and clothes on a makeshift rack between two ladders. My sister and her husband, Justin came from Philadelphia and painted my mother's bedroom and the eves of the house, while I took care of the garage sale. It was such a big help. I made everything very cheap. I found a realtor to list the house on the first of July. I hadn't realized that because I was Mother's guardian, that there would be a ton of paperwork and meetings before the sale could go through. The buyers actually made their offer on July first! That was the first day it was on the market! With Your intervention, dear God, the buyers were willing to wait an extra month for the paperwork to come through. Again God, You worked a miracle. Thanks for all the encouragement and pushing me to keep going when all I wanted to do was curl up in a ball on my bed. Thanks also for my friends and family that stepped up to help me. As I look back, I hadn't realized how much energy and patience my dad must have put in all those years. She could be funny and creative, on one hand, but angry and vicious on the other hand. The hard part was worrying about which emotion she would have next. I know this caused me a lot of anxiety and resentment. I was never sure. I learned to departmentalize my feelings.

Dear God, it's Me....Again,

Mother passed away.

We picked up mother's belongings from the assisted living facility that was her home for the past five years. We couldn't go inside because the pandemic was still raging. They had stuffed things in bags and boxes and put these on the concrete slab at the back of the building. My husband and three friends all came to help load it up. There were two vans, a car and a truck. It seemed sad that this was all she had left after ninety-one years of living. Of course, there was a lot of sorting, cleaning and trash when we moved her here, and when I got her house ready for sale. So here we are again. We loaded the furniture first. Some were spoken for and some would be donated to the local antique shop. The bags and boxes went into my garage for further sorting. Some pieces my friends took home with them. We got almost everything in two trips. Alan and I went back for the rest but sent my friends home with hugs and kisses. I had so many emotions. I was relieved she was not in pain anymore. I felt some uneasiness because I hadn't been able to visit her in two months. At the beginning of the pandemic, we could sign up for visits and talk to each other through a glass partition. As time went on all visitations stopped. Most of the residents as well as the staff had come down with Covid. Mother never did. I say she didn't die of Covid but of the loneliness and isolation that Covid brought. I had called the Director about a week before she passed, because she had stopped eating. I asked them to call the Hospice team. She could talk to me, but someone had to hold the phone to her mouth. Hospice people called me at four in the morning on January 20, 2020, to tell me it was happening fast. She passed before I could get there. She had signed up to donate her body to the Wright State College of Medicine. Her friend Wanda had learned about it, so they both signed up. I felt that was a very selfless thing she did for Science. We couldn't hold a service because of the pandemic. It all seemed so cut and dried. Maybe it was better for my mother and me to end this way. God I put her spirit and love in your hands now.

The End

Epilogue

My mother, Barbara, was born in March 1923. It was in the height of the Great Depression. Her mother was an employee of Goodyear and was having an affair with a man in management who was already married. After her birth, Barbara was cared for by her mother and her extended family. When Barbara was about four months old, her mother committed suicide. The family had no means with which to feed Barbara. She was passed around the family for about the next two years. She ended up in an orphanage in Cleveland. There was no money, and there were no jobs. It was a dark time in our history. Those early years were very hard on Barbara. She developed the awareness that she was unloved because she was always changing homes. She was there at the orphanage for another year or so until Walter and Laurel adopted her and made her their family. Her adoptive parents loved her and took very good care of her. It was them who I knew as Grandma and Grandpa. Mother had many mental illnesses and was on medications to help. She lived a long life and died in 2021. She is in heaven, happy and cured. I am so glad that our relationship with God helped her through life, and I know that her struggles were not her fault.

www.ingramcontent.com/pod-product-compliance
Lightning Source LLC
Chambersburg PA
CBHW021138130626
46554CB00005B/1568